3/22/69

Daniel —
    Keep building on the good
foundation you have.

            Shirley and Chet Braud

Adventure Into Architecture

John Quincy Adams was prophetic when he said "we must learn the arts of war and independence so that our children can learn engineering and architecture, and so that their grandchildren may learn fine arts and painting." The arts involve more than a leisure-time activity. We are interested in the arts because we have come to realize that they not only enrich but illuminate our lives; without them we are doomed to the monotonous rationality of a computer.

JAMES A. PERKINS, *President*
Cornell University

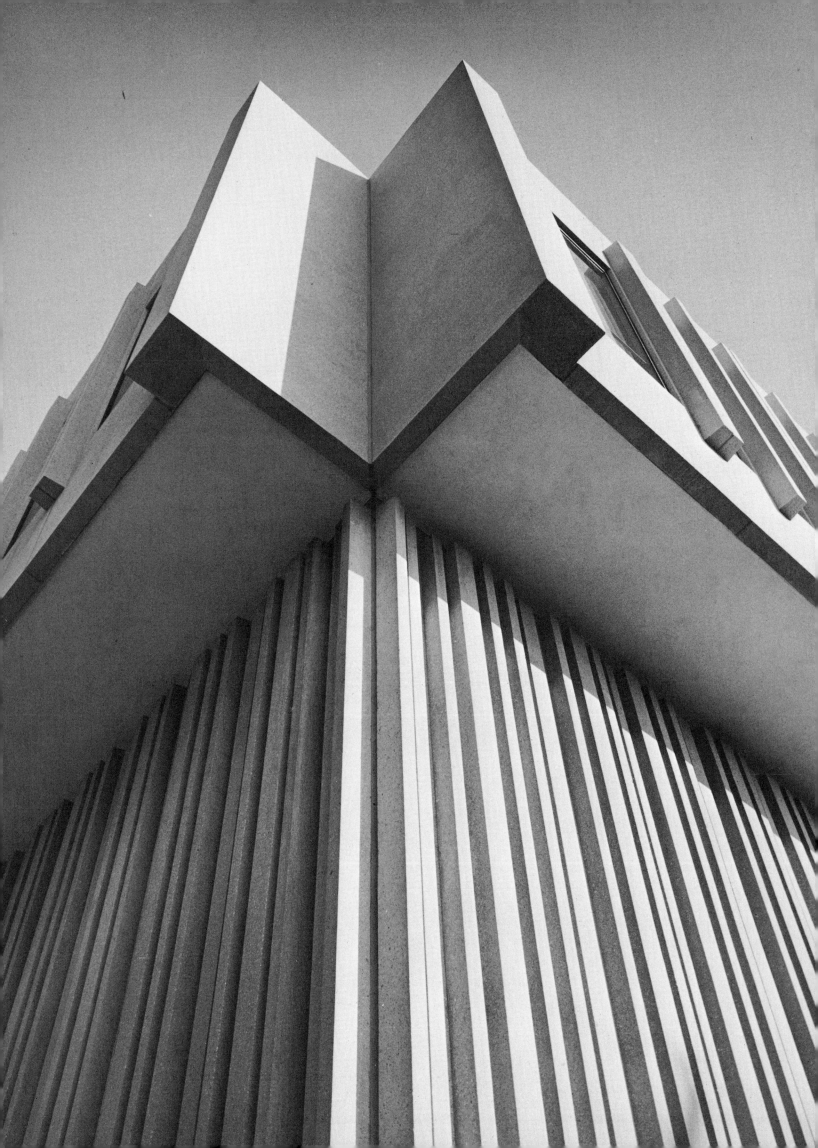

ADVENTURE INTO ARCHITECTURE

Bernard John Grad, F.A.I.A.

ARCO PUBLISHING COMPANY / NEW YORK

Published by ARCO PUBLISHING COMPANY, INC., 219 Park Avenue South, New York, N.Y. 10003 Copyright © Bernard J. Grad, 1968 All Rights Reserved. No part of this book may be reproduced, by any means, without permission in writing from the publisher, except by a reviewer who wishes to quote brief excerpts in connection with a review in a magazine or newspaper. Library of Congress Catalog Card Number 68–20406 Arco Catalog Number 668–01763–5. Printed in the United States of America. Book designed by Stefan Salter Associates

The author gratefully acknowledges the aid of Christine Debrowski, Janet Paust, Maria Calvano, Gail Wagner, David R. Dibner, Harry B. Mahler, and Howard N. Horii. These staff members of Frank Grad & Sons were most helpful in assisting the author with the research for this book. And to David Zugale, a special note of appreciation for his cartoons.

TO MARIAN, SUE, AND PETER

Preface

Here is a voice of experience telling you about our profession in entertaining fashion. Architect Grad is one of that generation whose practice has spanned the greatest era of change in the history of architecture, all packed into less than forty years.

He was educated when American architects were cautiously breaking out of traditional eclecticism; he has weathered the great depression and has experienced all of the revolutions in esthetic concepts, technology, business practice, and our current plunge into the complexities of the environment of a fully urbanized society.

Bernie Grad writes in the jargon of the profession. He is too steeped in it to do otherwise. This is good for the reader, I think, because we are all becoming adept at comprehending the babel of each others' languages in our specialized society and thereby share the intimacies of our separate philosophies.

This is truly an adventure into the world of architecture as it is today, with glimpses into the future. It is a world of art and business, government and industry, people and products, dreams and realities. You will be intrigued with it.

If you aspire to become an architect and do, chances are that you yourself will experience another fabulous era of change and opportunity. Chances are that you will find the career of an architect as fascinating as Bernie Grad obviously does.

W. H. SCHEICK,
Executive Director,
The American
Institute of Architects

Contents

Preface *by William Scheick*   7

Introduction   10

1. The Evolution of Expression   12

2. Education and Preparation   36

3. Major Roles of the Modern Architect   54

4. "The Establishment"   76

5. The Face of Construction   96

6. The Language of Vision   104

7. Infernal Eternities   128

8. A Typical Project—The New Jersey Cultural Center   138

9. The Challenge of Change   162

Introduction

This is not a history or a textbook of architecture; both needs have been amply and admirably filled. The purpose of this book is quite different. It is a primer and, hopefully, a source book written particularly for people interested in learning about the architectural profession.

With the increase in public and private construction necessary to meet the demands of the population explosion, more and more representatives of government, education, medicine, religion, business and private interests will come into contact with architects. This growth in urban renewal and suburban development presupposes the very real need for understanding between client and architect and, at the same time, highlights the importance of attracting more and more competent young people to the field of architecture.

If by examining the architect—his history, training, motives, the daily mechanics of his office, his very *raison d'être*—people can become more knowledgeable about him and his work, more good building should be the inevitable result.

The meaning of architecture goes far beyond the sterile definition offered by Webster: "The art or science of building." The Fourteenth Edition of the *Encyclopedia Britannica* is not much better in its interpretation. Architecture, the *Britannica* says, is "the art of so building as to apply both beauty and utility. . . . The problem that architecture sets itself to solve is how best to enclose space for human occupancy."

Neither definition is wrong, as far as it goes; however, both are incomplete. Architecture—which is both an art and a science—is the tool that creates environment, and hence, atmosphere and mood. Not only does it provide shelter and specific spaces for man's infinite needs, it directly influences people and their daily lives by guiding our work, play, education, research, religion, medical care, travel, and even our sleeping and eating.

For almost two centuries American urban, suburban and rural environments, and their intricate communications networks have mushroomed haphazardly to their present levels, stimulated by the driving force of materialism and expediency, and conceived in blindness and ignorance. The inevitable consequence—blight, decay, and strangulation—is only now being recognized and combated. We have at last learned that architecture must play a major role in reshaping this country's environment by replacing chaos with beauty and order.

What should make us sit up and take notice are these startling factors:

> There are only 30,000 registered architects in the United States, compared with 250,000 lawyers, 265,000 doctors, 430,000 accountants, and 975,000 engineers. The number of architectural firms is about 10,000.

> The population of the United States is expected to reach 300,000,000 by the year 2000. To meet the physical demands of this expansion, during the next 32 years, architects will be called upon to design as many facilities as Americans have constructed in the 192 years since the signing of the Declaration of Independence.

> Only one in every 100,000 people is being prepared to participate in the physical shaping of the nation's future. The 63 accredited colleges of architecture conferred 2,025 Bachelor of Architecture degrees, 417 Master of Architecture degrees and only 10 Doctorates—less than 2,500 degrees in 1966. A pitifully small annual task force to meet the staggering challenge of the immediate future.

We are truly the unknown profession, not only because our number is small. To many we are simply the creators of blueprints. Others have absolutely no idea what we really do in order to earn our fees. To nine out of ten clients and prospects, we are indistinguishable from the builders.

This mystery must be dispelled if Americans wish to uproot the ugliness and visual disorder that now surround us.

BERNARD JOHN GRAD, F.A.I.A.

1. The Evolution of Expression

Once upon a time, specifically from the era of Thomas Jefferson until the Depression of the 1930's, architecture was considered a gentleman's profession. It was practiced by the man who came from the right family, had gone to the right schools, made the right tours of Europe, learned the right things, and married the right wife. All of which is no longer true.

This concept is no longer valid because of the sequence of events and changes which have affected the lives of all of us. Since the early 1900's we have been involved in two world wars and several small skirmishes, some minor economic recessions, and a major depression, plus industrial, social, and scientific revolutions of great import.

So that you may better understand the architect and his work, let us look briefly at the climate, conditions, and circumstances of the late nineteenth and twentieth centuries in which he practiced. The social and economic forces to which an architect is subject will be readily recognized; the changes in these phases of our existence are so extreme that they are worthy of note.

During the last half of the nineteenth and the beginning of the twentieth centuries, the empire builders of America were at their apex. The whole country was building, changing, consolidating, and gambling. As fortunes grew, the towns and cities in which they were made mushroomed.

The emperors of industry, with European forebears, were conservative by nature and still under the influence of their mother countries. It was natural for them to demand conservative Renais-

NEW YORK PUBLIC LIBRARY. An adaptation of neo-classic architecture using Corinthian columns. Architect: Carrere & Hastings.
Photo by Gil Amiaga

Left

LINCOLN MEMORIAL. Greek Doric peripteral form, an outstanding example of neo-classic architecture. Architect: Henry Bacon.

Photo by Abbie Rowe. Courtesy of National Park Service

Right

JEFFERSON MEMORIAL. Circular temple adaptation with an extended portico, supported by columns of the Ionic order. Architect: John Russell Pope

Photo by Abbie Rowe. Courtesy of National Park Service

Left

VIRGINIA STATE CAPITOL. Roman temple prototype of the Ionic order. Architect: Thomas Jefferson.

Courtesy of Virginia Department of Conservation and Economic Development

Right

STOCK EXCHANGE. Neo-classic facade, strong in character, to symbolize the solidity of the American financial institution. Architect: Trowbridge & Livingston.

Courtesy of New York Stock Exchange

sance and classical copies for their homes, business establishments, commercial buildings, and banks. Gothic and, later, Victorian Gothic became the image of the cultural institution and the church. French chateaux and Tudor estates were the order of the day. If a business tycoon wanted a *palazzo* for a home, he ordered such a design from his architect.

Architects were retained to design buildings in which to make money, and homes and estates which would advertise their owner's wealth.

Like an athlete who worships only strength, Americans, in those years, believed only in what they called success; only success could enlist the services of the architect. The architect, on the other hand, could only create what he was allowed to create. Whatever his private visions, he could not, in practice, show his maturity until society was itself mature enough to recognize and accept it.

The majority of the architectural profession of the late 1800's and the early 1900's was not equipped to face the challenge of those days. Architects were as divided in their philosophies as the society of which they were a part. The copies they created are living evidence of their temporizing—an adaptation of the past.

The first manifestation of American architecture began to take form at the end of the nineteenth century in the skyscraper. It was the natural result of the tempo of the times: migration, nationalism, technological innovations, and industrialization.

The architect became, in the public mind, the creator of commercial symbols. The most obvious symbol, for those who could afford it, was the tall building. Esthetically, it was still a reflection of a historical period, a vertical elongation of the Greek, Roman, or Renaissance style.

With the industrialization of America, warehouses and factories multiplied, in most cases without the benefit of architectural services; offices, commercial structures, and tenements were built wherever the economy dictated. The cityscape grew uglier, and the countryside was marred because of this lack of direction.

Particular attention was given, however, to the "front doors" of our cities. The beginning of the twentieth century was the time of the City Beautiful movement. The gateways of our cities became monumental, characterized by Washington's Union Station (1904), New York's Pennsylvania Station (1906), and Grand Central Station (completed in 1913). Once again, all were designed in the classic tradition.

Top

RESIDENCE OF MR. EDGAR S. BAMBERGER. Influence of English architecture on a suburban residence. Architect: Clifford C. Wendehack.

Bottom

RESIDENCE OF MR. EDSON BRADLEY. American residence of the Tudor style. Architect: Howard Greenley.
Photo by Gil Amiaga

ISABELLA STEWART GARDNER'S FENWAY COURT. Venetian *palazzo* in
New England. Architect: Willard T. Sears.

New York Life Building. Architect:
Cass Gilbert.
Photo by Rudolph Associates

METROPOLITAN LIFE TOWER BUILDING.
Architect: Jacques LeBrun.
Photo by John Gregory

Two examples of the elongation characteristic of Renaissance architecture.

GRAND CENTRAL TERMINAL. European influence on architecture of American railroad stations during the early part of the 20th century. Architect: Warren & Wetmore; Reed & Stem.
Courtesy of Penn-Central Railroad System

PHILADELPHIA MUSEUM OF ART. Typical of many museums and libraries constructed in the early part of the 20th century, this structure employs the Greek architectural form. Architect: Borie, Traumbauer & Zantzinger.
Photo by A. J. Wyatt

In all of our cities, museums, libraries, opera houses, theaters, and city halls were examples of the Renaissance and classical forms rising to express a way of life—but forms only—rarely functional in design.

Cities were proliferating, but vertical growth alone was given serious consideration. In the first three decades of the 1900's, technology took precedence over architecture, and, consequently, the period lacked variety of originality and boldness of architectural concept.

One has only to observe the monotony of our federal architecture to become aware of the uniformity caused by the fear of deviating from the norm of conservatism.

During the Depression, the number of registered architectural firms dropped by half, and the average annual volume of business of the survivors was reduced by 75 percent.

The thirty years that followed brought World War II, two violently repressive, authoritarian revolutions, and the invention of instant holocaust.

Out of all of this came but one agreement by architects: the machine must be accepted. From this concept, which had its birth in the German school of the Bauhaus, came the first stirrings of contemporary architecture in the United States.

Men like Ludwig Mies van der Rohe and Walter Gropius had fled Hitler's Germany and emigrated to America. Here they gathered their architectural disciples and developed an architecture adapted to the world of machines, radios, and fast motor cars.

Their foremost principle was to express structure, at the expense of all else. They felt that structure, above all, must be honestly and clearly revealed. From this emphasis on structure, contemporary, or modern architecture was to evolve.

Out of World War II and the postwar boom came the society's recognition of the need for architects, not only to design individual buildings but to rescue old cities from strangulation and to plan new ones. Industry and business began at last, to recognize their own stake in architecture.

The federal government also took a position heretofore avoided. Almost clandestinely, in the early 1950's, the State Department sponsored designs by eminent American architects, permitting them latitude in their skills and tasks, to design embassies abroad.

In 1957, stimulated by such men as Representative Frank Thompson of New Jersey, some Congressmen began to perceive the

CHAPEL AT RONCHAMP, FRANCE. Plasticity in architecture so aptly defined in this concrete structure which could be timeless in its origin. Architect: LeCorbusier.
Photo by Ezra Stoller

DEPARTMENT OF THE INTERIOR, WASH-
INGTON, D.C.
Courtesy of General Services Administration

Adaptation of the basic architectural
orders for government buildings.

VAN NELLE FACTORY, ROTTERDAM. The
emergence of modern architecture in
Europe as a result of the influence of the
Bauhaus School. Architect: J. A. Brink-
mann and L. C. van der Vlugt.
Courtesy of Netherlands Information Service

obligation of government to foster and strengthen the arts. This
benefit to architecture became a reality when former President John
F. Kennedy appointed a special ad hoc committee to assist the
government in obtaining the services of competent architects who
could design in the modern idiom and bring new life and spirit to
the national capital.

Headed by former Secretary of Labor, Arthur Goldberg, the
committee was instructed to carry out a study and prepare a report
on *Guiding Principles for Federal Architecture.** This document
may prove to be the finest stimulus for the profession in this country's history; for what was approved for Washington would set the
standard for public architecture throughout the country. The committee's report was brief but cogent.

The government, it pointed out, is under no obligation to be an
innovator in architecture, but it does have a positive duty to avail
itself of the finest contemporary architects and architectural thinking. "The design of federal office buildings, particularly those in the
capital," the committee declared, "must meet a two-fold requirement: efficient and economical facilities, and visual testimony to the
dignity, enterprise, vigor and stability of the government." To this
end the committee recommended a three-point policy:

1. Requisite and adequate facilities must be provided in a distinguished architectural style and form. Designs must embody the finest
contemporary architectural thought. Specific attention was focused on
the possibility of incorporating qualities that reflect regional architectural
traditions. Designs should follow sound construction practice, buildings
should be economical to construct, operate and maintain, and should be
accessible to the handicapped.

2. At all costs the establishment of an "official style" must be avoided.
Design must flow from the architectural profession to the government,
not in reverse. The advice of distinguished practitioners should be solic-
ited before the award of important design contracts.

3. The choice and development of a building site should be the first
step in the design process. Special attention should be paid to the en-
semble of streets and public places of which the proposed building will
be part. Wherever possible, buildings should be so located as to permit
the generous development of landscape.

* Ad hoc Committee Report. Available from Government Printing Office,
Washington, D.C.

SALK INSTITUTE FOR BIOLOGICAL STUDIES, TORREY PINES. Recaptures the hilltown architecture of Italy. Architect: Louis Kahn.
Photo by Marvin Rand

On opposite page

SEAGRAM BUILDING. Outstanding example of a beautifully articulated window-wall expression. Architect: Mies van der Rohe and Philip Johnson.
Photo by Gil Amiaga

These guide lines were heartily approved by the profession as a whole, for they opened the way to the kind of situation in which the contemporary architect works most happily.

Because of better understanding and unprecedented cooperation, we are now beginning to see the results of the sacrifice of private to communal and urban interests.

In many cities, renewal and revitalization are now taking place. Pittsburgh, Boston, Philadelphia, Baltimore, Denver, Hartford, Washington, Detroit, Chicago, San Francisco, as well as many small cities and towns now see that money spent on beautifying the environment is not wasted, but in fact can make a tangible return on the investment.

Today, however, we are still groping for an expression of American architecture. We have learned that there is a limit to functionalism: the mere expression of a building's use does not make a work of art. The profession is once again fragmented, and creative architects are striking out in diverse conceptual efforts.

Mies van der Rohe and his followers still pursue the school of "less is more."

Pier Luigi Nervi makes use of monumental, curved, geometrical, concrete forms.

Edward Durell Stone enhances the unification of a composition by designing an overall decorative screen to envelop the structure.

Le Corbusier and his disciples liberate form in the use of plasticity in concrete.

The "Ruins" school designs piles of concrete forms which look like inverted ziggurats and are reminiscent of Mayan temples.

The "Bump" school expresses rooms and spaces by hanging them outside the walls.

The "New Brutalism" school aims at making a startling statement in architecture by sheer boldness and mass.

The "Hill Town" school presents a philosophy of design reaching back to the Italian hill towns of the Middle Ages.

The statements in the style used by Yamasaki in both high- and low-rise buildings employ a graceful expression of "Contemporary Gothic" forms.

In the opinion of most architects, this variety of direction is healthy: all is not lost. Sometime in the future we will have a general direction disciplined by logic and requirement.

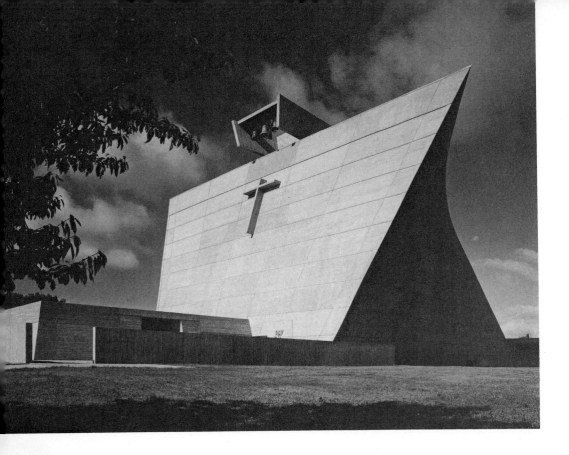

Top

St. Francis de Sales Church. This boldly expressed statement in reinforced concrete makes the architect's work recognizable. Architect: Marcel Breuer and Herbert Beckhard.
Photo by Hedrich-Blessing

Bottom

Woodrow Wilson School of Public & International Affairs, Princeton. The delicate use of concrete, employing Gothic forms, a characteristic which appears in many of Yamasaki's works. Architect: Minoru Yamasaki & Associates.
Photo by Joseph W. Molitor

Top

MINOR SPORTS PALACE, ROME. A gem of a concrete building executed by the "master builder"—architect, Nervi. Architect: Pier Luigi Nervi.
Courtesy of Architectural Forum

Bottom

CLARK UNIVERSITY LIBRARY BUILDING. Exemplifies the so-called "bump" school in which the architect has expressed on the exterior the spaces within the building. Architect: John M. Johansen.
Photo by Louis Checkman

The challenge is clearly stated in *The Architecture of America
—A Social and Cultural History.*

How is the architect of today and, even more, of tomorrow to be
educated so that, retaining his esthetic intuitions unblunted, he will know
enough to plan wisely and to coordinate the counsels of those who, as
specialists in the many fields within which he must operate, must be
called in to advise him? Can the architect trust his personal intuitions
when his work becomes involved with matters of complex social behavior? If he cannot, can he ever learn to be good enough simultaneously
as economist, sociologist, psychologist, engineer, political scientist, and
even demagogue and still retain his entity as an artist? If, as reason
clearly indicates, such a prospect is the worst of chimeras, can the architect survive as an artist, much less remain as the coordinator of building?
Can he really, as a member of a team, deal competently with urban
enterprises of the magnitude now demanded without losing all touch
with human reality?

In 1968 the good architects know that they are not yet ready. What
they must decide—and, even more, what their successor generation in
the art must resolve—is whether the architects can ever be ready or
whether they must yield to the package dealer who designs, builds and
even finances, and who is even less ready but who does not hesitate to
offer his gilt for gold.

Unready—but far from unwilling—we admit we are; but what
concerns us next is what we are doing to make our heirs ready to
carry our art beyond the millenniums of development so rapidly
sketched here.

* John Burchard and Albert Bush-Brown. *The Architecture of America—
A Social and Cultural History* (Boston: Atlantic-Little, Brown, 1961), p. 508.

BOSTON CITY HALL. Prime example of the inverted ziggurat form. Architect: Kallmann, McKinnell & Knowles; Campbell & Aldrich; Le Messurier Associates, Inc.

2. Education and Preparation

In the past hundred years, the phenomenal growth of architecture in the United States is even more amazing when one considers that American facilities for architectural education are themselves barely a hundred years old. It was in 1869 that the first independent course in architecture was established at the Massachusetts Institute of Technology. Until then, the only means of qualifying as an architect in this country was the pupilage method inherited from Britain. Under this system, the aspirant served a long apprenticeship under a practitioner who taught him while he worked: analogous to the traditional practice of "reading law" in a lawyer's office that was gradually eliminated by the growth of law schools.

Until the inauguration of the architectural course at the Massachusetts Institute of Technology, there had been no academic instruction in architecture except in a few trade schools where design was taught as part of the science of building. The precedent set by MIT was slow in developing: by 1898 it had been adopted only by Harvard, Columbia, Cornell, Syracuse, the Illinois Institute of Technology, George Washington University, and the Universities of Pennsylvania and Illinois. In that year, these schools along with MIT, had a total enrollment of 362 students of architecture. This is a startling contrast with the figure of twenty-two thousand students in the sixty-three schools of architecture recognized by the National Architectural Accrediting Board in 1968. (There are almost twenty other schools that have not been accredited; hence, their graduates are not included in this figure.) See Appendix for list of accredited colleges.

In the first thirty years of this century, virtually every school of architecture followed the same procedure. The student was first exposed to the grammar of the profession, taught by the use of the *analytique*, studies in proportion and the elements of architecture. The use of the French names for this and other aspects of the course was not accidental; it reflected the almost exclusive dominance of the École des Beaux-Arts of Paris, about which we shall have more to say presently. All of the student's work was initiated by an *esquisse*, a preliminary sketch to be made in a fixed time—usually nine hours spent *en loge*, that is, in isolation in an individual booth. The proportions of an *esquisse* might later be varied, but all the elements shown in it had to appear in the final *analytique*.

It was at this stage that the student was supposed to master the various orders, or major styles, of architecture, and study the great monuments held up for his edification in his books. He was taught to draw first in pencil, then to trace in ink with a ruling pen using Chinese ink. Finally, there was the *rendering*, which modeled the forms by showing shadows cast by a sun that conveniently always hung at a forty-five degree angle to the horizontal.

Conventionalism ruled. Armories and prisons were Romanesque or Gothic fortresses; banks manifested their character, strength, and stability through the use of Greek or Roman styles. Design was dictated by the iron hand of tradition. An additional shackle was imposed by a predominant interest in geometry of form without regard to use or cost. In teaching, the technique of graphic presentation received greater emphasis than the more important courses in design. This unrealistic kind of "paper architecture" marked the worst of American Beaux-Arts work, and led to at least one ironic incident in my own student days at the University of Pennsylvania.

Each university that subscribed to this Beaux-Arts system sent to the Beaux-Arts Institute in New York those projects to which it had awarded its own prizes. These were exhibited at the Institute headquarters in New York City; every month or so there was a judging. It soon became apparent that most of the medals went to the students most adept at rendering their designs in brillant, eye-catching style. It took awhile for the university professors to realize that as many as six or seven hundred projects were being judged in a single night. Simple arithmetic showed that the jury could spend no more than fifteen or twenty seconds in examining each submission, which explained why the awards went to the submission with unusual eye appeal. If the student violated the rules of the system by radically changing his *esquisse*, he was immediately ruled *hors concours*, out of competition.

When one Pennsylvania student was barred, despite the fact that his design was a fine solution to the problem posed, our faculty was stunned. An investigation disclosed that he had been excluded only because the jury could not believe that any mere student was capable of producing such a brilliant rendering. The university officials were so incensed that they offered to send the student into the office of any one of the jurors and dared them to give him a project on which he could not turn out a rendering that would be the equal of the one that had been condemned. The challenge was not taken up.

In retrospect, it must be conceded that the unreality of the Beaux-Arts system was not incompatible with the times in which it held sway: the wealthy wanted old-world magnificence, in utter disregard for contemporary needs. The architectural student was devoting himself to the study of a temple of love, a problem in superimposed classical orders, a Mediterranean casino, an American embassy in Asia, a palace in a great capital, while his society was erecting factories, office buildings, and schools.

Every reputable architectural school in the country was headed by a Frenchman. Many of these men were serious teachers and excellent designers, but unanimously they centered on classical architecture. They understood little about the social and intellectual ferment in the country in which they were living.

Each profession had its measure of outstanding graduates. In law, election to the position of editor of a university's Law Review signifies the top honor a student can achieve; in architecture, the winning of the Paris Prize was the signal honor coveted by architectural students. This reward financed a two-and-a-half year continuation of studies at the École des Beaux-Arts in Paris and established the goal for every architectural school in America. Consequently, the universities were constantly competing for the various French architects teaching in this country and, for a time, there was a constant migration of leaders and their staffs from one university to another. Cornell's staff transferred to Yale; the University of Illinois lost its faculty to Columbia; New York University set up an atelier whose prime purpose was to produce a Paris Prize winner. Not only did this inter-university rivalry preclude any real continuity of teaching, but the emphasis on the Paris Prize distorted the whole curriculum.

The Beaux-Arts system was concerned predominantly with in-

ARCHEO. Archeological project done by the author in 1929 at the University of Pennsylvania. This "Greek Temple" is a typical example of an *analytique*, a composition in which the major elements used in the design are enlarged to form the frame at larger scale.

dividual buildings. It offered no courses in site planning, city planning, or master planning; its students were not to concern themselves with any knowledge of transportation, economics, or sociology. Design was the highest good—indeed, the only good; social and economic problems were utterly ignored. Nor was much more attention given to structure.

In the 1930's, at the University of Pennsylvania, only a mall divided the School of Architecture from the College of Engineering —a physical mall and a figurative abyss. This separation was hardly bridged by what was called—when given any thought at all—"gut courses." These were supposed to teach the viscera of a building: plumbing, heating, ventilation, air conditioning, and electricity. The average student simply came to class once a week, sat as close to the rear of the room as possible, and suffered the instructor to read from a book. No one studied, no one could have passed an examination. But none was given, hence, no one flunked.

Despite all the criticisms of the Beaux-Arts school—and many are irrefutable—one cannot deny that it was the best that our educational system could offer at the time. In spite of being steeped in tradition, a good number of us were strongly interested in the modern work being done in Europe and for which we had to find our own technical training.

Our refusal to accept unquestioningly what was doled out to

GREEK and ROMAN ORDERS of ARCHITECTURE

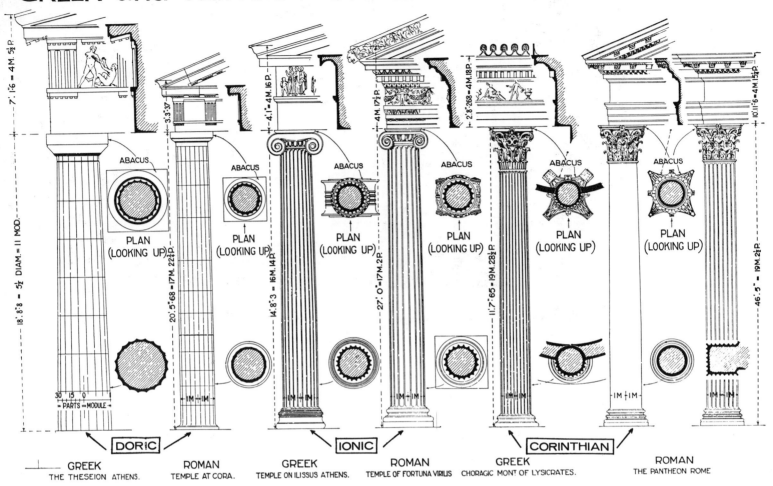

NOTE: A module equals half the lower diameter and is divided into 30 parts

us, our insistence on looking farther on our own initiative, was no isolated phenomenon. Well aware of the fallibility of generalizations and equally skeptical of accepting statistics blindly, it is interesting to refer to a recent study conducted in an effort to isolate what makes an architect. It is not unsafe to argue that most of those who choose a particular profession, for reasons other than money alone, necessarily have certain common characteristics that respond to the allures of the field they have entered. This study corroborated my own empirical observations of almost forty years.

Without exception, it was found that the architect has at least one parent of artistic inclination, if not of considerable skill. Almost without exception, the architect himself displays a substantial aptitude for drawing and painting. In school, he tends to be a fairly

EDUCATION AND PREPARATION

GREEK AND ROMAN ORDERS OF ARCHITECTURE. Columns, architraves and pediments of the Doric, Ionic and Corinthian orders shown in their respective modular proportions.

good—but not outstanding—student. The major college-days' characteristic of the architects who were included in the survey was their intellectual independence. As a result, they could be classed as respectable B students who could and did turn out A+ work in fields that aroused their interest, but who were quite content to vegetate through courses that did not excite their imagination. As students, they were profoundly and rationally skeptical, not readily awed by faith or authority alone, but, in general, not rebellious merely for rebellion's sake. There is a clear impression that they feel they learned the most from those who were not easy with them. And, though the adjective is one to be handled with forceps, in these days of facile rhetoric, the average architect may be said to be dedicated to his work.

In these times, he must be dedicated if he is to succeed at all. The architect can no longer be thought of—or think of himself—as an amiable dilettante assured of a gracious life by catering to the fancies of a few more or less cultivated individuals of means. On the contrary, today's architect—and even more tomorrow's—works for all men everywhere, and for this reason: his is the most social of all the arts, and his profession is increasingly affected by the public interest. Today's architect, by recognizing his opportunities and responsibilities, can make a major contribution to his society, or by default, he can do irreparable damage.

The Architect Defined

I like to think of the architect as the analogue of the conductor of the symphony orchestra, who must guide, coordinate, and harmonize the many diverse people with whom he works. The architect's first responsibility is to his client, which is most often, today, a committee; the conductor's responsibility is to the association that has hired him. The conductor must translate a musical score and its rendition by many instruments into an auditory whole; the architect must translate the program or the requirements of his client, through the direction of many associates, into a design concept. Like the conductor, who must be familiar with all the techniques of instrumentation, the architect, in the modern world, must have far more than a passing knowledge of engineering, finance, economics, sociology, and psychology. A young man or woman, who believes that one can be a competent architect without proficiency in these fields, would be well advised to consider some other profession; without the capacity, or the will, to become a many-faceted individual, one will never be more than half an architect. For those who can accept self-discipline, the rewards in pure satisfaction of achievement cannot be measured.

Classically, the architect is defined as a creative artist. This does not mean that architecture has room only for genius; not all men, and not all architects, are truly creative. There are, in fact, three categories of architects.

The first is that of the innovators, those who see architecture as a continuum of experience. They can project themselves into the future and provide a glimpse of a probable architectural development in relation to the evolving social, cultural, and technological environment.

The second and largest category is that of the practitioners who, seeing and comprehending the work of the creators, although they cannot necessarily match it, find that they can incorporate part or all of it into the immediate environment. These are the normal working architects who, understanding the idiom of the times, are interested in producing good architecture and who, by their concerted efforts, shape the general environment.

The third and smallest group holds the rare breed of architect who wants a non-practicing career. He is the man sought out by the building industry, government, educational institutions, publications, trade associations, and by large corporations that want architects in their "in house" management. In daily matters, his work is close to many aspects of practice, except that he is never engaged in the creative processes of design.

This three-pointed challenge of today is quite different from that of past generations. In the early 1930's, no one wanted an architect of any category. Five years before, I had been one of a class of fifty-five freshmen, of whom only fourteen graduated. The casualties of the Depression accounted for some of the mortality, but most of it, as in any professional school, was the result of the inevitable weeding-out process of the years. Of the fourteen who graduated, exactly three are practicing today; it is no coincidence that each of us was the son of a practicing architect. Yet every one of those fifty-five freshmen had been convinced of his vocation to the creative aspect of architecture. Many of those who dropped out or were forced out, like many of those who graduated, found their roles in the non-practicing areas of the profession. This was by chance; for at that time there was nothing like today's demand for architects outside the field of practice.

Our constantly changing, contemporary world now calls on the architect for what the profession calls "expanded services." Here the architect faces the challenge of programming buildings and their uses, preparing basic programs for all kinds of projects, leading and carrying out research into needs and requirements, site investigation, real-estate analysis, and comparative market studies.

The new recognition, that attention must be focused on the community as a whole, necessarily compels architecture to revise its concepts of design in terms of all the prevailing socio-economic forces.

Often the architect is called on to design interiors and their furnishings and equipment. Occasions are multiplying in which a client wants his architect to perform high managerial functions, and management engineering becomes one of the architect's proliferating roles. Every sign indicates that the future will make even greater and more varied demands on the profession.

Evolution in Education

For the architectural student, evolution in institutional preparation has been slow. The curricula of most schools of architecture, until perhaps a decade ago, were very nearly alike. In the 1930's, a typical architectural curriculum was basically a five-year course. It consisted of two years of the humanities and basic architecture and three years' concentration on purely architectural subjects. The first part was almost identical to the first two years of the liberal arts curriculum—embracing mathematics, basic sciences, languages, and literature—but adding basic architecture, elementary design, the history of architecture, descriptive geometry, perspective, shades and shadows, strength of materials, and all the other fundamentals that could be compressed into the two years. In theory, these two years would enable the student to determine whether he was truly suited to the profession. Some found their greatest strength was in mathematics and engineering, while some soon learned that they were really artists. Thus, without too much loss of time, the first group could transfer to engineering or other scientific schools, and the second could devote itself to the fine arts. However, those who demonstrated proficiency in the subjects that specifically tested their abilities in architecture, spent the next three years concentrating on that alone. In the end, they graduated as bachelors of architecture.

Some institutions offer a compromise between the traditional five-year undergraduate course and the trend of the past decade toward a six- or seven-year combined curriculum that makes the architectural degree a graduate-school function. MIT, for example, has established affiliations with as many as twenty-five other colleges in order to provide two simultaneous degrees after the completion of five years of study. Under such plans, a student, who has completed three years of liberal arts study at, say, Amherst, spends the next two years at MIT studying only architecture. He then receives a baccalaureate in arts for his Amherst work and another in architecture. Columbia, while also treating architecture as an undergraduate school course, has a four-year course that requires at least two years of previous liberal arts study and, frankly, gives preference to applicants who have baccalaureate degrees in the arts or sciences.

This preference of Columbia's is a prerequisite of those institutions that have sharply defined architecture as a graduate study. Architectural applicants at such schools must have a thorough grounding in the humanities and the social sciences, buttressed by elective courses bearing directly on the profession. These institutions believe such students to be better prepared for a more under-standing and exclusive study of architecture, during their two, three, or four years of graduate work.

In those institutions where architecture is an undergraduate school, the student's exposure to subjects not intrinsically architectural is necessarily limited—I would say too limited. In his five years he must master all the elements that are generally considered to be part of a well-rounded education, all the practical subjects influencing his profession, and, in addition, all the fundamentals of architecture. It is somewhat analogous to expect an aspiring lawyer or doctor to complete a seven- or eight-year education in five years. Necessarily, the emphasis will be on the purely professional courses, and the student is almost bound to emerge with dangerous gaps in his related knowledge. When, on the contrary, he can spend four undergraduate years perfecting his understanding of the society in which he will work and the forces that will be both his allies and his enemies, he is infinitely better equipped to devote the following three years to his profession.

SHADES AND SHADOWS. Problem—cast shadows in plan and elevation in this project done at Pratt Institute.

SHADES AND SHADOWS. Solution—shows the shadows cast at a 45 degree angle.

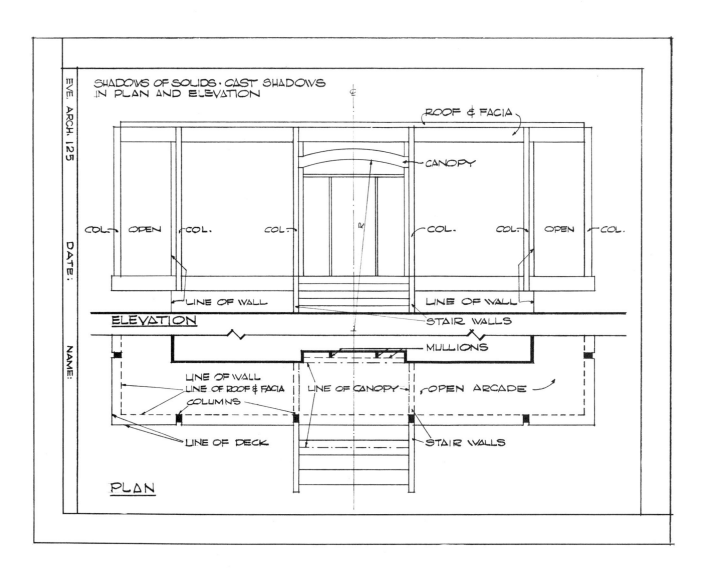

SHADOWS OF SOLIDS · CAST SHADOWS
IN PLAN AND ELEVATION

ROOF & FACIA

CANOPY

COL.   OPEN   COL.   COL.   COL.   COL.   OPEN   COL.

R

LINE OF WALL   LINE OF WALL

ELEVATION

STAIR WALLS

MULLIONS

LINE OF WALL
LINE OF ROOF & FACIA   LINE OF CANOPY   OPEN ARCADE
COLUMNS

LINE OF DECK   STAIR WALLS

PLAN

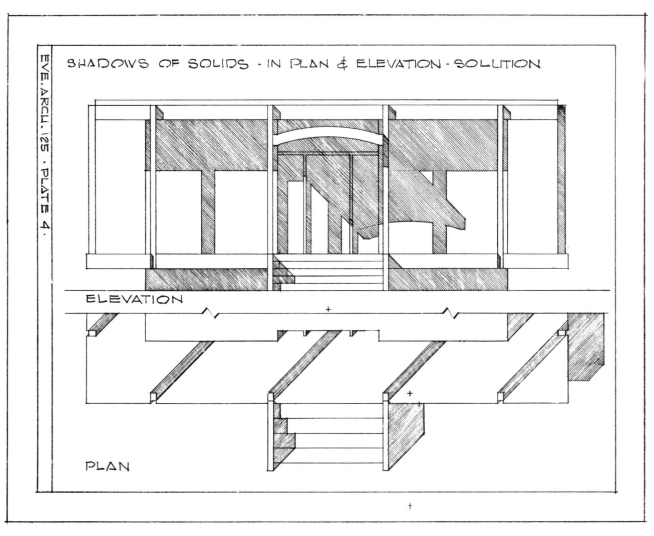

SHADOWS OF SOLIDS · IN PLAN & ELEVATION · SOLUTION

ELEVATION

PLAN

To say that I whole-heartedly endorse change in this direction is to understate my position. The supposedly old-fashioned, classical education is an absolute prerequisite for a finished architect. Knowledge and understanding of the humanities, the sciences, and particularly the social sciences is of prime importance. For the architect, nothing is irrelevant, whether literature or geopolitics. He must learn as long as he lives, and a genuine, classical education will, more than any other preparation, make him both able and eager to spend his life educating himself beyond what his university has done for him.

The University of Pennsylvania is one of the forward-looking institutions that has established a three-year curriculum in a graduate school of architecture. In addition to the usual undergraduate studies, entrance requirements include one year of drawing and one year of basic design. The three-year graduate course is worth examining in some detail.

The student's first year is devoted to six subject areas. The first is the study of architecture as a social art; an art based on and, in turn, influencing society. This naturally encompasses the architectural and landscape elements that contribute to the environmental quality of a neighborhood—schools, housing, playgrounds, parks, and shopping and community centers. The second course concentrates on contemporary thought and its relevance to current professional problems in designing urban environments. The much broader course in theories of architecture discusses the influence of materials, techniques, function, and scale on architectural form and includes critical analyses of examples by leading contemporary practitioners. This study in turn, is a logical coordinate of the course in principles of architecture, which covers the guiding principles of design, program analysis (the analysis of the various uses of the building and its components), and the relationship of function, structure, and construction methods to space.

At the same time, the first-year student must take an exacting course in drawing, in which his exercises in the graphic representation of form emphasize shades, shadows, perspective, and the techniques of renderings, with particular stress on the relationships between space and structure. Finally, he is introduced to the theory of structures. He starts with the principal factors in the design of a structure as a whole, goes on to form as a function of structure, and concludes with the elements of the structure: the factors that produce stress; the paths taken by loads within structures; the natural and mechanical properties of building materials; stresses and strains; loads as mechanical forces; the simplification of systems of forces; the application of mechanical principles to the design and elements of structures; analytical and graphic methods for determining stresses in structures and their elements.

The second year's six courses are no less arduous progessions from the fundamentals of the first year: architecture; materials and methods of construction; structural steel and timber; reinforced concrete; he echanical equipment of buildings; and the electrical equipment. The titles are not glamorous, but without the fundamentals there would be no durable art. Architecture, as a course (it is continued in the third year), is a series of critical examinations and analyses by the school's studio masters and by visiting critics of architecture. It is the only course of the year in which there is a subjective element, and it is vital to the esthetic shaping of the student. The study of materials and methods of construction embraces: the uses of lime, cement, steel, concrete, masonry materials and lumber; foundations and masonry walls; light and heavy wood framing; choices of materials—steel, non-ferrous metals, reinforced concrete; the various components of the building—roofs, floors, doors, windows, stairs; the preparation of working drawings; and, finally, the choice of construction methods. Structural steel and timber is a lecture-and-problem course on the practical application of theory to structural parts, such as timber construction, steel framing, walls, beams, girders, columns, trusses, various types of roof and floor construction, and fireproofing. The lecture-and-problem method is also used for the reinforced-concrete course, which deals with theory and its application to various types of slabs, beams, girders, columns, walls, footings, and stairs. The two equipment courses cover heating, air conditioning, water supply, plumbing, drainage, and all the electrical problems of a modern building.

In his third year, the student continues the critical seminars begun a year earlier. His other courses are theories of architecture, new methods of design and construction, professional practice and specifications, and one elective that may be chosen from the whole range of the university's courses. Most important of all, he must prepare and submit his thesis for graduation while he is engaged with his required and elective studies. Theories of architecture are both historical and analytical. Establishing an identification of art, especially the art of architecture, includes: classic, formal, and mathematical theories of architecture, the predecessors of the modern movement, the current changes in taste, the orientation of art criticism, technological development, social changes, esthetic theories, contemporary thinking on the arts in general, and the evolution of architectural thought—all of which, for the serious and imaginative student, is at once a gold mine of learning and an inexhaustible stimulus to original thinking.

At the same time, his feet are kept on the ground by the study of new methods of design and construction, which deals with ultimate design, prestressed concrete, rigid frames, flat plates, folded plates, thin shells, suspended structures, and space frames. The course in professional practice and specifications is no less important; for here the student comes to grips with the vital questions of professional ethics, building finance, contracts, building codes, office administration, and the form and content of specification-writing. The most important activity of this final year is the thesis. Largely independent, original work, the thesis is based on a program prepared by the student himself. Both the project and its execution will largely determine his qualifications to be an architect. He must submit the architectural details, the structural and mechanical drawings, and the computations and specifications relevant to his project. It will then be judged not only for originality, but for competence.

A 1967 survey by *Progressive Architecture* states that in the last few years it has become increasingly apparent that architectural education is in a state of turmoil.

Within three years, twenty-three men have become heads of their own or other schools, and about 80 percent of the schools have instituted significant changes in their curriculum. Of the sixty-three accredited schools, thirty have switched to a six-year program.

The survey reports "a whole new generation of students learning that questions are more important than answers, that process is more important than product, that the architect is more than a form-giver, that architecture is more than a series of individual movements."

Such changes naturally breed controversy, and during any controversial period many changes will take place. New educational ideas will be attempted, evaluations made of their effectiveness, and modifications will then result. In its attempt to meet the challenge of turning out better architects, more qualified to meet the complex problems of tomorrow's world, revisions in our educational system will provide the means to increase the number of graduates and may well mean that the profession itself will change radically from its present status.

All this I explain in detail, glossing over none of the hardships, on every occasion when I am bearded by some would-be architect in quest of counsel. Each time I am amazed by how little knowledge most of them have about the profession—but I suppose, really, that the generations are not so dissimilar in this respect. I can recall quite a number of fellow-freshmen in 1927 who had chosen the School of Architecture for purely alphabetical reasons. Another never-ending source of astonishment to me is the unqualified lack of manual dexterity and ability to draw in so many of the aspirants, virtually all of whom are thinking of becoming purely creative architects. Anyone, who is at all serious about architecture as a profession, should first develop the ability to draw, paint, and build models if he has it. If he lacks these skills, his future in the field is not encouraging. He must be able to sketch, to translate conceptual thoughts into graphic forms immediately understandable to other people.

It is not inappropriate to emphasize that architects, trained to converse graphically with one another, often find it difficult to understand that the average layman cannot instantly, or even ultimately, read a drawing—especially one that is technical. He can pretty quickly comprehend anything with a three-dimensional quality but it is the very rare layman who can understand a plan even when it is being explained to him. So often people go on nodding to me, assuring me that they understand while I go over plans with them; I am convinced that, if there were no written words to identify the various parts of the plan, one could explain it upside down and they would still profess to understand.

Most untrained people simply cannot understand graphics that are made primarily for communication between professionals, and this is hardly surprising. The professionals must be able to make graphics for their lay audiences. One West Coast architect trained himself to draw upside down; he could sit opposite a client at a desk and simultaneously draw and explain verbally.

If he wishes to enter a worthwhile university, the would-be architect—besides cultivating a graphic talent—must have finished as close as possible to the top of his secondary-school class. But these two prerequisites are far from sufficient to pave any (nonexistent) royal road to success: there are non-academic preparations that are just as essential. The future architect must develop an interest in, and an awareness of, building construction and the physical facilities that surround him. He should get a summer job on a construction project and see the physical process of putting together a building; an after-school job in an architect's office will help him to absorb the atmosphere and learn the mechanics of the office operation. He should make every effort to travel in order to observe what is done, and how it is done, in other cities and, if possible, in other countries. In the process, whether he travels around the world or can afford to go no farther than the next city, he should recognize that his choice of a profession imposes on him the obligation of being particularly aware of what goes on round him, because his is the profession of shaping environment.

He should also read in secondary school, during vacations, in college, for the rest of his life. As much as the alert physician or lawyer, the successful architect must keep himself constantly abreast of the literature of his profession, both at home and abroad. It is axiomatic that his preparation should include mastery of at least one modern language, if only in order to read what his foreign colleagues have to say. Fortunately, for those who lack the linguistic flair, an increasing number of architectural publications are multilingual.

"Freely ranging in a good library," *American Education* has observed, "an inquiring mind can seek nourishment in the recorded ideas of men belonging to far distant times and places. There it can choose among scores of teachers, boldly explore the vast diversity of human thought and base its own conclusions upon centuries of evidence."

By the year 2000, experts predict, every building now standing in the United States will have had to be duplicated because of the growth in population and the accelerated rate of development and advancement. What a contrast to that June of 1932 in which my class of fourteen graduated!

Today's graduate, as a rule, has spent at least one summer in an architect's office and made contacts in his home city or in some larger one that attracts him. If he has not, he has only to look at the advertisements in any metropolitan newspaper. As a bachelor of architecture, he can expect to start work at approximately $7,500 a year; if he has a master's degree, he can command a better beginning wage. This beginning is not a license to practice. Most states require a period of apprenticeship, usually three years, quite analogous to that served by the law graduate in a preceptor's office or by

LIBRARY, MONMOUTH COLLEGE. Contemporary addition to a classical form, one style acting as a foil for the other. Architect: Frank Grad & Sons.
Photo by Gil Amiaga

the medical graduate as a hospital intern. Obviously, the design of buildings involves the safety, health, and welfare of the public; hence, the architect, like the other professionals similarly involved, must supplement his theoretical training with practical experience before he can safely be qualified to practice his profession, however well he may have scored in the license examination now required by all the states.

It is rare that the young architect, having completed his apprenticeship and received his license, will be ready, or even willing, to set himself up in private practice. Most young practitioners, whether they work in large, middle-sized, or small firms, prefer to gain more experience and deeper knowledge of every facet of the profession before they go out on their own. The apprentice years involve far more than the basic technical knowledge of how to design a building, how to put it together, how to prepare the working drawings and contractual documents suitable for contractors to bid on. This so-called "in-house" knowledge is only part of the mental capital that the young architect must accumulate.

He must learn how to obtain commissions ethically, how to maintain client relationships, how an architectural office collaborates with the vast construction industry and its complexities of general contractors, subcontractors, manufacturers, vendors, and distributors of building materials. He must familiarize himself with the various governmental agencies that have jurisdiction over his work, with the requirements of building codes, zoning laws, and labor regulations. Whatever the project, it will often include dealing with planning boards, renewal directors, and industrial and art commissions. When all these have been satisfied, there are still the insurance underwriters, whose rules and judgments can doom a design and, similarly, the clients who insist on strict conformity, and the others who are willing to pay penalty insurance premiums in order to take advantage of an unusual feature. Thus, it is evident that the practice of architecture is not merely accepting a client's program and translating it into a design concept.

Like most offices, we try to infuse new blood into our organization on a regular basis. One source is the employment of college or even high school students during their summer vacations. In many cases a student will spend two or three summers with us and then join us as a regular employee after graduation. The two or three year period he spends serving what may be called his apprenticeship is analogous to the internship period of the young doctor.

Just as the young medic goes through all of the medical services of a hospital including medicine, surgery, pediatrics, obstetrics, gynecology, etc., so the young architect is exposed to the five aspects of the practice of architecture—design, working drawings, specifications, construction, and administration.

I had an interesting question asked of me by a 16-year old prep school junior on whom I tested the manuscript of this book. He asked, "How do I get to be the coordinator or the leader of the band —and by what steps?" The answer, of course, is by going through all of the stages of practice and becoming so proficient in one or more areas that his leadership shows.

If his college career has developed him as a designer, the young architect's talents will be recognized in any office and he will either start as a junior designer under the direction of a superior—or if he has been on the board as a draftsman, part of a team developing the working drawings of a project—by his own output—his design abilities will be evident. Good firms are interested in people who think; for only they who think can create. It matters little in which slot a new employee, fresh out of college, starts his career. If he has talent it will show.

Ours is a profession that requires a practical as much as a formal education. The young architect must learn how to put a building together so that it not only is a pleasing sight and serves the purpose for which it is created—but it must work properly. When the young architect demonstrates his drive to become a leader, he is automatically shepherded in many directions. His exposure to all facets of architectural practice is planned by his superiors to complete his practical education. Without the ABC's of good construction practice—conformity to codes and regulations, knowledge of basic materials—too many young designers fall on their faces by creating buildings that cannot be built. An idea is only good if it can work.

Let's not forget that all of us are not creators—most of us in fact are not. Therefore, the majority of architects spend their time in the other important activities of the profession.

I have previously referred to the basic talent which I believe to be so important to the successful architect—the ability to express oneself graphically. But this I do not mean that unless an aspirant to the architectural profession can draw or paint, he cannot become a good architect. But by doing so, his chances are much greater for success. Permit me to clarify this much-misunderstood subject. The ability to express oneself graphically does not mean that an individual is an accomplished artist or delineator. The ability to do competent mechanicals and freehand drawings is a great asset. Similarly knowing how to paint, in oils, watercolor, or tempera, strengthens the architect's conceptual designs.

Many offices, ours included, make only rough studies of design sufficient for study and development. Final presentations are farmed out to professional renderers.

The force that motivates and strengthens the apprentice, throughout his long indenture, is his creative drive. He is collecting an architectural vocabulary for its best expression. He is enlarging his own creative talent by research. He is studying the newest tools and techniques available, as well as the work of colleagues and competitors. Enriched beyond the resources of his professional ancestors and their few natural materials, he will be constantly studying the accretions of his working capital represented by new products and new uses. Metaphorically, he will be preparing for his own debut as that symphonic conductor whom I mentioned earlier.

3. Major Roles of the Modern Architect

Today's practicing architect must be as much a businessman as a professional and an artist. Whatever the size of his office, he must have the training and the capacity to manage it. An architectural office must operate within a defined budget and support itself on fees that represent a fixed percentage of the dollar value of its production. Thus, the architect's ability as a management executive assures him of deriving a profit from his work and providing a healthy financial foundation. In short, in addition to architectural design capability he must be able to design a profit.

"In-house" Operations

Within the profession, the basic office facilities and activities are called the "in-house" operations. These are the same whether·the office consists of three people or a hundred; the only difference is whether each person has to do one job or several. Most architectural offices choose to confine their work and their personnel to those talents that are specifically related to architectural design. Other, equally necessary services are rendered by consultants whom the architect engages on a project basis.

"In-house" operations are directed by the executive architect or architects—the partners in the firm, the men concerned with fundamental policy-making and management. Immediately below them and essential to the execution of their decisions is administration, an individual or a group, without which the office would disintegrate.

Of equal rank with the administrators are the architects and designers who make up what might be called the conceptual staff. They are the creative directors of the office. Next come the project managers, non-designing architects who head the teams or groups involved with various projects, and the draftsmen, who together with the project managers form the *production team*. The draftsmen may be aspiring architects or general working architects, brand new graduates or veterans of the profession who find their greatest satisfaction in executing the ideas of others. In any case, they know construction details and the technique of delineating them. They know how, under the direction of the job captain, to take drawings from the basic design or schematic stage, and develop them into precise drawings that can be read by the craftsmen in the field who actually build the structure from these working drawings.

Here I have postulated as many people as tasks. The number of tasks never varies, though the size of the office will determine whether each is carried out by a different man or whether John Smith may not be his own draftsman and/or job captain in addition to having designed the project.

The working drawings are always accompanied by the contract specifications, prepared by the specification writers. This classification is misleadingly narrow. The textual documents they prepare (as distinguished from the drawings produced by the draftsmen) may be as thick as two Manhattan Telephone Directories. They minutely describe the nature of the materials to be employed, where, and how they are to be used. The contract specifications put into words what is not portrayed in the drawings and also explain the graphic delineation of the project. They are, in addition, a legal instrument, forming part of the contract between the owner of the building and the general contractor. Hence the men who put together these specifications must be much more than technical writers. They are researchers, consultants with manufacturer's technical representatives; and are responsible for the working vocabulary of the architect's office with respect to available building products.

No matter how small, every architect's office must have the ability to monitor construction. Its function is the observation of the actual building work. First of all, its checkers meticulously inspect the shop drawings submitted by manufacturers. These shop drawings specify the dimensions of each component part of the building in great detail, they are the means of making the parts fit together into the whole.

In sum these are the fundamental "in-house" architectural operations that bear directly on the realization of a project. A more detailed elaboration of such other necessary "in-house" functions as how the architect obtains work, how he programs and budgets it in his own office, how he creates a *persona* for his office and his abilities that he hopes will attract clients, how he projects himself and his office into the community in order to contribute to the common good will be discussed in later chapters.

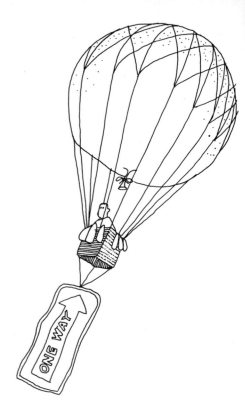

Phases in Design and Execution

The "in-house" activities that are restricted to the execution of projects can be divided into three major technical categories:

1. The conceptual planning and design phase is the responsibility of the architects and designers who must translate the client's program into the schematic and preliminary phases of the work;

2. The production stage involves the development of the preliminary drawings into the final working drawings and contract specifications, which are the architect's instruments for obtaining competitive bids or negotiating with contractors and from which the building is actually constructed;

3. Finally there is the construction phase, during which the architect and his representatives observe the builder's work in order to make certain that construction complies with the contract.

Consultants

Throughout these three periods the architect will be working with and through more than a dozen consultants:

The first, *the surveyor,* is usually retained by the architect's client to provide an accurate delineation of the site. The survey gives the dimensions of the property and includes a complete topographical description that shows contours, trees, shrubs, and rock outcroppings. The survey pinpoints the location and size of all surface and sub-surface utilities such as sanitary sewer, storm sewer, water, gas, and electric supply. Telephone lines are also located. If any of these services are not available at the site, investigation is undertaken to determine the nearest available supply.

When a site is subject to heavy traffic, *transportation experts* are consulted.

Next, the architect will call upon *experts on soils* and sub-soils, who will determine the bearing capacity of the site to support the structure planned for it and the influence of these characteristics on the problems of the foundation, including the sub-surface water level.

A *real estate consultant* will analyze the rental economics of those projects that depend on tenancies.

Short- and long-term financing of the project is the field of the financial or *banking consultant*.

When the project involves sales potential, *market analysis experts* are summoned.

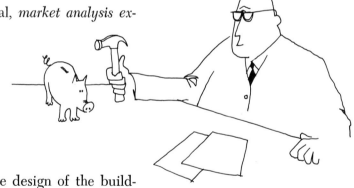

Structural engineers are required for the design of the building's structural components.

On complex projects, *site planners* and landscape architects play an important role.

The *space planner* is particularly useful to government and large corporations; for his expertise in analyzing current and future space requirements can be most helpful to owners who do not have their own personnel trained in this important function.

Interior design consultants are retained if the architect's "in-house" talents do not include such experts.

 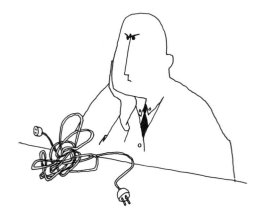

Mechanical and *electrical consultants* will determine the heating, air conditioning, plumbing, and electrical requirements.

Illumination experts will execute special interior and exterior lighting effects.

In more and more large structures, *food service consultants* are creating facilities for dining rooms, cafeterias, and snack bars.

Acoustics will be entrusted to *acoustical engineers.*

Cost control and systems consultants work with the architect in the design stage to help establish budgets and controls and must remain on call until the project is completed.

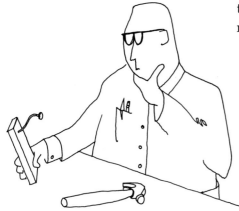

Some special projects will require the assistance of *research institutes*.

Testing laboratories must analyze all the materials to be employed in the building.

Finally, there are the technical services of manufacturers, whose experts are consulted on the desirability and practicability of the multitude of products manufactured in the United States and abroad.

A Hypothetical Project—from Concept to Completion

How the architect is able to bring these diverse talents and abilities into harmony is best illustrated by following the development of a hypothetical project, from its inception to the day when the client accepts the finished building. Taking full advantage of the leeway one enjoys in hypothetical situations, we will assume that the client knows exactly what he wants.

STEP ONE—*Program Analysis*. The client presents the architect with a clearly worked-out program that specifies his building's purpose: who will occupy it; what activities are to be carried on within it; is it to be a complete entity in itself, or is future expansion contemplated and, if so, in what manner. Where no program exists, the architect is frequently called upon to develop this schedule of requirements, with the help of his client. The formulation of this program is a prime factor in the success of a project because it defines the present and future functions of the building complex. It is basic to integrated design which must always be governed by outside practical considerations. The architect cannot merely create space and form and then tell each of his consultants to fill them in independently. Everything must be designed as a single homogeneous entity so that all parts of the building function together.

STEP TWO—*Schematic Design*. The architect's next task is to translate the program into a functional design, that is, to express the written word graphically. This phase of the work involves many aspects. It begins with the development of an orderly arrangement of *space relationships* within the structure and the placement of the building on the site.

A building is always designed from the inside out, and the space relations are decided by the various activities to be carried out. They are usually studied through what architects call *bubble diagrams*. A bubble diagram contains a series of circles or squares, representing the building's planned functions, so worked out that the architect can easily understand the interrelations of the individual spaces. The bubble diagram is, in effect, a *work-flow chart* as well. In a factory, for example, it automatically becomes a chart of the processes, from the arrival of raw material to the shipment of finished goods; in an office building, housing a giant firm, it serves to map the course of the paperwork that is the sole activity.

FLOW CHART USING CRITICAL PATH TECHNIQUES

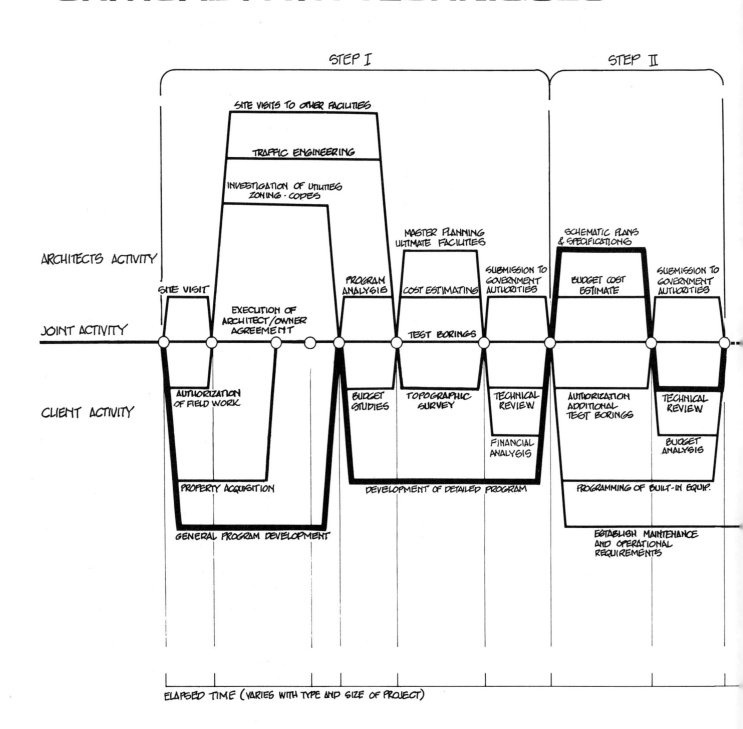

STEP I

STEP II

SITE VISITS TO OTHER FACILITIES

TRAFFIC ENGINEERING

INVESTIGATION OF UTILITIES
ZONING · CODES

MASTER PLANNING
ULTIMATE FACILITIES

SCHEMATIC PLANS
& SPECIFICATIONS

ARCHITECTS ACTIVITY

SITE VISIT

PROGRAM
ANALYSIS

COST ESTIMATING

SUBMISSION TO
GOVERNMENT
AUTHORITIES

BUDGET COST
ESTIMATE

SUBMISSION TO
GOVERNMENT
AUTHORITIES

JOINT ACTIVITY

EXECUTION OF
ARCHITECT/OWNER
AGREEMENT

TEST BORINGS

CLIENT ACTIVITY

AUTHORIZATION
OF FIELD WORK

BUDGET
STUDIES

TOPOGRAPHIC
SURVEY

TECHNICAL
REVIEW

AUTHORIZATION
ADDITIONAL
TEST BORINGS

TECHNICAL
REVIEW

FINANCIAL
ANALYSIS

BUDGET
ANALYSIS

PROPERTY ACQUISITION

DEVELOPMENT OF DETAILED PROGRAM

PROGRAMMING OF BUILT-IN EQUIP.

GENERAL PROGRAM DEVELOPMENT

ESTABLISH MAINTENANCE
AND OPERATIONAL
REQUIREMENTS

ELAPSED TIME (VARIES WITH TYPE AND SIZE OF PROJECT)

System of plotting the interactions between architect, client, and contractor. The eight steps described in the text are subdivided and charted on a time basis. All of the architect's activities are indicated above the line and the client's below the line.

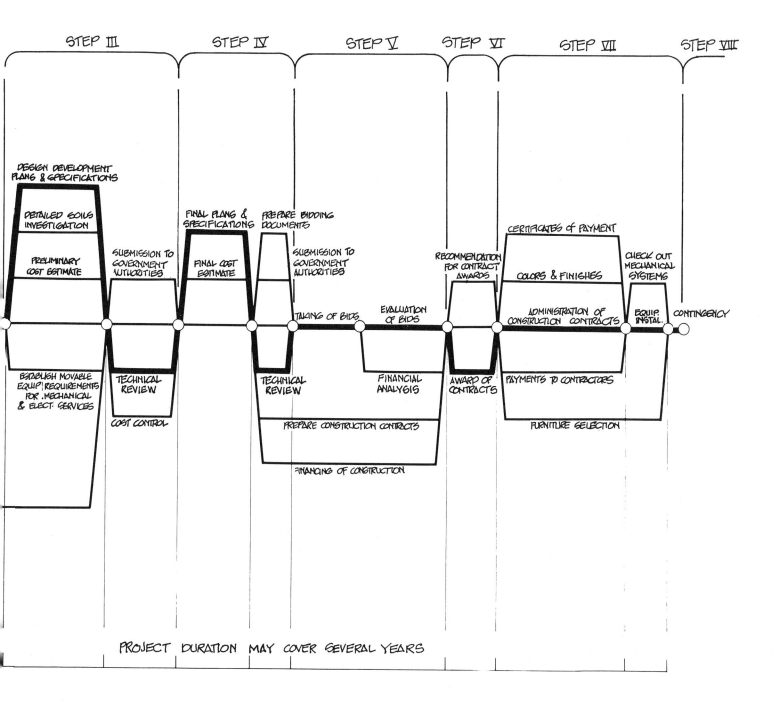

Along with the development of spatial relationships is the *site study*. This phase of the work relates the architectural concept of the structure to the site, the topography of which is canvassed to give the building design the advantage of the best site possibilities. Sub-soil conditions are explored by examining and evaluating boring samples, and soil-bearing capacities are established. The architect considers orientation of the building with regard to solar relationships. He relates the project to its neighbors. The contour, drainage problems, and views of, and from, the site also bear on his design concept. An important part of the study must be the various transportation facilities to be accommodated on the site. Lines of flow must be developed for employees, parking, visitors, vehicles, raw materials, finished products, and often rail and recently even helicopter traffic!

At this stage of development, many other pertinent aspects are investigated. Conformity to governmental, insurance, and other requirements must be considered from the moment of undertaking the program. The architect must be certain that at no point will he involve anyone in a violation of law. In constant consultation with the client and with the small army of consultants incessantly feeding material into the design concept, the architect must exhaustively study all applicable *building, zoning,* health, and labor laws, *insurance regulations,* and any other prescriptions or proscriptions that will influence his final design.

It is only when the program, the space relationships, the site study, and the regulatory requirements have been thoroughly coordinated can the architect really begin to design. In delineating the first basic concept of the building in schematic drawings, he begins with the inside of the structure. Very often these will be supplemented by *small-scale, rough models* to permit three-dimensional study. Obviously, the first scheme that comes into the architect's mind will not always satisfy either what he has in view or what the client prefers, and it may be necessary to redesign again and again before both the architect and the client approve the result. But let us assume that this stage has been reached, our hypothetical client being both extremely knowledgeable and very easy to please.

In addition to the schematic drawings produced, the architect's office has now to prepare an *outline specification*. This defines the materials to be used and the structural system to be followed. The types of mechanical, electrical, plumbing, air conditioning, and lighting systems are established and delineated in preliminary form.

Interior finishes for floors, walls, and ceilings, and whatever special effects may be required by the client's program are similarly studied and selected.

The last element in the schematic design package is a statement of the *probable cost of construction*. At this stage it usually consists of an estimated square-foot cost applied to the area of the building.

STEP THREE—*Design Development*. Once the schematic design studies have been reviewed and approved, the architect's next effort is the development of this concept into a well-defined, articulated building. In this phase of the work, detailed drawings and other data covering building characteristics, environment, structural, mechanical and electrical systems, materials, and other essentials are developed. The goal of the architect is to complete his preliminary package—a set of drawings sufficiently detailed to describe the project graphically. These drawings are many: floor plans to show space relationships in all the component parts; sections through the building, to show the heights of the floors and the general nature of the structural design; all exterior elevations, with the materials to be used; sometimes, there will even be drawings of actual furniture and fixture arrangements. These drawings are dimensioned in sufficient detail and are usually summarized with a tabulation of the total square foot area and cubic foot volume.

The architectural design development drawings will be accompanied by others showing the structural concept. Mechanical drawings will portray the types of heating, air conditioning, plumbing, electrical systems and all the mechanical components of the building. There must also be a site plan, showing the relation of the building to the total site and to all the utility services that must be connected in order to give the building life. A preliminary landscaping plan will delineate trees, shrubs, lawns, and parking facilities.

The *rendering* in full color is always part of the preliminary package. Very often, there will be a scale model of the completed project to give the client his own three-dimensional view. This is especially valuable when the client is a committee, at least one of whose members may not be skilled in apprehending the perspectives of even the finest rendering.

Now, for the first time, the architect has at hand all the data he needs in order to take a good, hard look at costs. The preliminary budgeting phase is quite as important as the architect's esthetic concept; for if both are not consonant, his project is out of tune. It is always gratifying if the client knows as much as the architect about

"ON TARGET" COST TECHNIQUES

COST TARGET

PROGRAMMING STAGE

Client establishes $;
Architect establishes
basic design parameters.
                or
Client establishes needs;
Architect establishes $.
....
In either case Client and
Architect <u>must</u> be in agree-
ment on design parameters
and construction cost
budget.

COST ESTIMATING TECHNIQUE

Experience of Architect in
translating design para-
meters into a $ per sq. ft.
of buildings and site

DANGER POINTS

Wishful thinking on $ per
sq. ft. and anxiety to show
owner a "favorable" budget.

COST TARGET NO. 1 ESTABLISHED

COST TARGET

SCHEMATICS STAGE

Architect translates design
parameters into single line
"departmental" plans,
sketch elevations and construction material lists.
Consultants prepare description of mechanical and
electrical systems, kitchen
equipment, etc.

COST ESTIMATING TECHNIQUE

Architect applies refined
$ per sq. ft. costs to
buildings and site; consultants do same. Allow
contingency 5-10%.

DANGER POINTS

Reluctance of Architect to
face reality if Target #2
is missed on high side.
If this happens, project
<u>must</u> be cut back.
....
Client is advised of
adjustments required to
plans to stay "ON TARGET".

COST TARGET NO. 2 MATCHES NO. 1

One method of exercising close control over the costs of a project. In every stage maximum precaution is taken to control costs and to inform the client of any changes that would have an impact on the budget.

COST TARGET (3)	COST TARGET (4)	COST TARGET (5)
DESIGN DEVELOPMENT STAGE	**CONTRACT DOCUMENTS STAGE**	**CONSTRUCTION STAGE**
Architect translates Schematics into larger scale detailed plans, elevations and sections. Consultants make single line overlays on Architect's plans plus layouts of critical mechanical areas. Outline specs prepared.	Architect translates Design Development into working drawings and specs; consultants do likewise.	"Normal" job conditions and minor A/E oversights may eat up contingency.
COST ESTIMATING TECHNIQUE	**CONSTRUCTION COST TECHNIQUE**	**CONSTRUCTION COST TECHNIQUE**
Outside cost consultant and M & E consultant, Kitchen equipment consultant, etc. make detailed take-offs at about 90% completion. Architect reviews critically. Allow contingency 1-3%.	Outside cost consultant makes detailed take-off of general construction; consultants take off own. Architect reviews take-offs and pricing critically. Allow contingency 3-5%.	Examine contractor's "extra" claims with care.
DANGER POINTS	**DANGER POINTS**	**DANGER POINT**
Reluctance to change almost final contract documents; additional client requirements creeping in; overlooking construction market condition prevailing at anticipated bid time. . . . . Client is advised of adjustments required to plans to stay "ON TARGET".	Many small spaces become apparent on plans; M & E systems are too sophisticated; special client requests are made. . . . . Client is advised of adjustments required to plans to stay "ON TARGET".	Changed client requirements.
COST TARGET NO. 3 MATCHES NO. 1	**COST TARGET NO. 4 MATCHES NO. 1**	**COST TARGET NO. 5 MATCHES NO. 1 UNLESS ABOVE DANGER POINT OCCURS**

construction costs. If, for instance, a client, wanting 100,000 square feet, knows that for the kind of building he has in mind he must expect a cost of $20 per square foot, he will not balk at the architect's budget of $2 million. But far too often clients have champagne tastes on beer budgets. Not knowing how much their buildings will cost, they have made unrealistically small appropriations. Since the architect is not a magician and does not control the prices of materials and the wages of workmen, he must enlighten his client as to the extent of the gap between what he would like to have and what he has allocated the funds to buy. Such discrepancies are especially frequent when the ultimate user of the building is a division of a corporation or an agency of government, for in most cases the appropriation for the project has been fixed by some other division of the company, or agency of the government, in which the user has little or no voice.

If the disparity is not resolved at this stage, disaster is inevitable. No architect can deliver two dollars' worth of building for one dollar, even when he finds a program thrust into one hand, a budget into the other, and he receives the curt instruction to make them match. When he is dealing with people who understand, or can be made to understand building costs, the problem is not so acute; but when his client lacks both competent advisors and prior building experience, or is a governmental unit with a fixed appropriation set by a legislature, the architect must hold fast and make it clear that the client has only two choices: to accept the architect's realistic cost appraisal and to fund the project accordingly, or to revise the program drastically enough to fit within the appropriated budget. Matters are never eased by the inevitable, gratuitous advice of friends who have heard of an identical building in Podunk that cost infinitely less than the architect says this one will.

Here is where the architect must be able to document every word he says and to communicate intelligibly with his client. He must recognize that no layman has been trained to understand either his vocabulary or his wordless language of drawings. The architect is well-advised at this point to warn the client that, however accurately he has figured, actual bids may show a range of as much as 20 percent from low to high bidder. He must insist on the validity of his own previous experience and of the corroborative evidence of cost consultants who can verify his explanations to the client.

But our pleasant hypothesis postulates quick agreement on

costs if only for the sake of furthering our illustration.

To complete the preliminary package, the architect submits his complete analysis of budget and probable costs. It is preferable that the whole package be presented for discussion at a full-scale meeting with the client and his principal advisors. Questions can then be answered on the spot with reference to the visual material at hand, and any graphic presentation can be explained as soon as it is questioned.

STEP FOUR—*Construction Documents.* Approval of the design development package signals the development of final working drawings and contract specifications, on the basis of which bids are invited. All the parts of the building are portrayed in final scale, immediately understandable to all the people who will have to study these documents and build from them. As these documents progress, they are checked and cross-checked so that all phases of the architect's, engineer's, and consultant's work may be integrated into a co-ordinated whole that will facilitate the contractor's actual work. Cost controls receive special emphasis, for the client can change his mind at any time during the development of the project. If his suggested changes increase his costs above the figures that he approved with the preliminary drawings, the fact must be drawn to his attention. It is not solely for the client's benefit that so much attention is being given to money: The wise architect sets a check-rein on himself and his consultants lest the project run away with itself. The final cost estimates are presented to the client with the final drawings and specifications, very often a new scale model, and illustrations of the building as it will look upon completion. Approval of the final package means that the job is ready for bidding.

STEP FIVE—*Bidding or Negotiation.* This is not the place to explore the manifold complexities of the construction industry: these we shall save for a chapter of their own. Here I should like to limit myself to the mechanics of bidding on a construction project. When government is the client, the procedures are controlled by statutes, which allow contractors to bid in answer to published advertisements and individual invitation. These bids must be competitive, in compliance with government standards. In private work, the manner of bidding is jointly decided, as a rule, by client and architect.

Theoretically, competitive bidding makes it possible for an infinite number of contractors to seek any given contract; but in practice most projects draw bids only from contractors in the vicinity. Only the very largest contracting firms move about the country in search of work; a few maintain offices in several major cities, and a very few reach overseas.

The general practice, with respect to a private project, is that client and architect agree in advance on a list of possible bidders. This is based on their own knowledge of, and experience with, these contractors. Once the list is drawn, the architect first ascertains that the firms named will be willing to submit proposals. He then sets a date on which they will receive copies of all the contract documents, with instructions for the preparation of their bids and a final date for submission. In general, the bids are sealed. While those on government projects are opened publicly, a private owner need not follow this example.

Upon submission, all bids are tabulated and analyzed by both the client and the architect. Government projects are automatically awarded to the lowest bidders who have complied with the bidding instructions. On private projects, the client and the architect usually agree on the low bidder, although special circumstances may lead to the selection of another contractor.

On occasion, an owner elects to omit the bidding process and engages a contractor to build his project. In most cases, the contractor guarantees an upset ceiling price and is paid a fixed fee, which is negotiated between the owner and the contractor.

Step Six—*Award of Contract.* The successful bidder is then called in to receive his instructions. In our office, we generally invite him to a meeting that includes our client. This provides the opportunity for further discussion, planning a schedule of work, and clarifying any details that the contractor may wish elaborated. The contractor is also given an outline of the procedures that our office has set up and include, primarily, methods of submitting progress schedules, breakdowns of the costs of each of the building trades involved (enabling the architect to approve or modify the contractor's monthly requests for payment), systems for approving subcontractors, specified materials and shop drawings, a method of submitting payment requisitions and, finally, a firm schedule of periodic meetings at the construction site where representatives of all parties —owner, architect, contractor, and major subcontractors—can review progress and co-ordinate work.

Step Seven—*Administration of Construction Contracts.* General administration by the architect throughout the time of construction cannot be over-valued. Whether he will always be accompanied by the client during his periodic visits to the site to review the progress and quality of the work will depend largely on the latter. The number and frequency of such field trips will vary with the circumstances of the project. So will the size of the architect's representation: on a simple building, one man may be quite enough; observation of large or complex projects is very often made by a staff representing not only the architect but the structural, mechanical, electrical, and site engineers. The purpose of such trips is simply to assure conformity to the contract documents.

The architect does not supervise the work, but based on his on-site observations he will endeavor to guard the owner against defects and deficiencies in the work of the contractor.

Long before the first field trip, the architect has had to begin his review of *shop drawings*. This is a continuing task which ends only when the building is completed. These are drawings of the thousands of parts that go into any structure. They are submitted by the general contractor, his subcontractors, and the manufacturers and vendors who supply the actual parts. The architect checks each drawing for conformity to the contract drawings and specifications.

The completion of the building means the final, formal inspection by the architect. It is by no means his final visit, however. When the contractor notifies the architect that he has completed his contract, the architect, the owner, and all the consultants or their representatives converge on the building and go through it from bottom to top in order to make certain that the contractor has fulfilled his obligations in accordance with the drawings and specifications. This having been established, the architect accepts the building and certifies it to the owner. The contractor is paid his final balance, and the appropriate governmental agencies then inspect the building. When they have certified it for occupancy, the owner takes it over.

STEP EIGHT—*Follow-Up.* For the next year the architect schedules periodic visits to the building. Practically, these are not absolutely necessary; psychologically, they have a considerable value in showing the client that the architect has a continuing interest in his work that is not extinguished by final payment of his fee.

To list these eight steps, from the receipt of the client's program to the certification of the building, has taken rather less time than to carry them out. Naturally the layman wants to know how much working time the average project requires—especially the layman who is paying for the architect's time and talent. Unless the project is a single-family house or an unusual crash program, the answer may surprise not only the man with the checkbook but the eager novice who has just bought his first drawing board: two to three years.

Generally, there is a lapse of six months to a year between the time when the architect receives the original program, or is retained to assist in its preparation, and the completion of the working drawings and contract specifications for potential bidders. The actual building will usually require a year; if the project is big enough, the time may well be doubled.

Our own organization is probably not atypical, and perhaps its make-up and *modus operandi* would be useful as a kind of general illustration of professional organization. Our staff totals approximately one hundred people, and is best described by this organization chart.

In addition, there are the guest soloists, the consultants who serve any number of architectural orchestras. Only a very few architectural offices, are so large that they find it more economical to have many or all of the consultant services "in-house." This is rarely advantageous. For ten years we experimented with a hybrid form of the two systems, maintaining our own structural engineering design department and a small mechanical engineering department, but we found that we made much better architectural music at lower cost when we relied on visiting soloists. Today we regularly use many consultant firms in structural, mechanical, electrical, and air conditioning phases of our work. Long collaboration has resulted in so close a relation with these soloists that we almost consider them part of our own orchestra.

This provides the flexibility of being able to select, for a given job, a consultant whose experience may be much better adapted to the client's needs. In addition, we were able to take advantage of the tides that occur in the diverse consultant's work-loads.

Every good architectural office has one department that I have not yet mentioned: research. Its field is the constantly fluid one of new methods and materials. For almost five thousand years, until the sudden burgeoning of the industrial revolution, architects and builders had worked only with the few basic materials provided by nature. Today they work chiefly with the products of man's own ingenuity. This constantly accelerating technological advance has produced so many new materials and methods and has so increased

The chart indicates how the relationship between client and architect starts with two people, builds up as the various stages of the project are executed, and ends with the same two representatives.

CLIENT-ARCHITECT RELATIONSHIPS

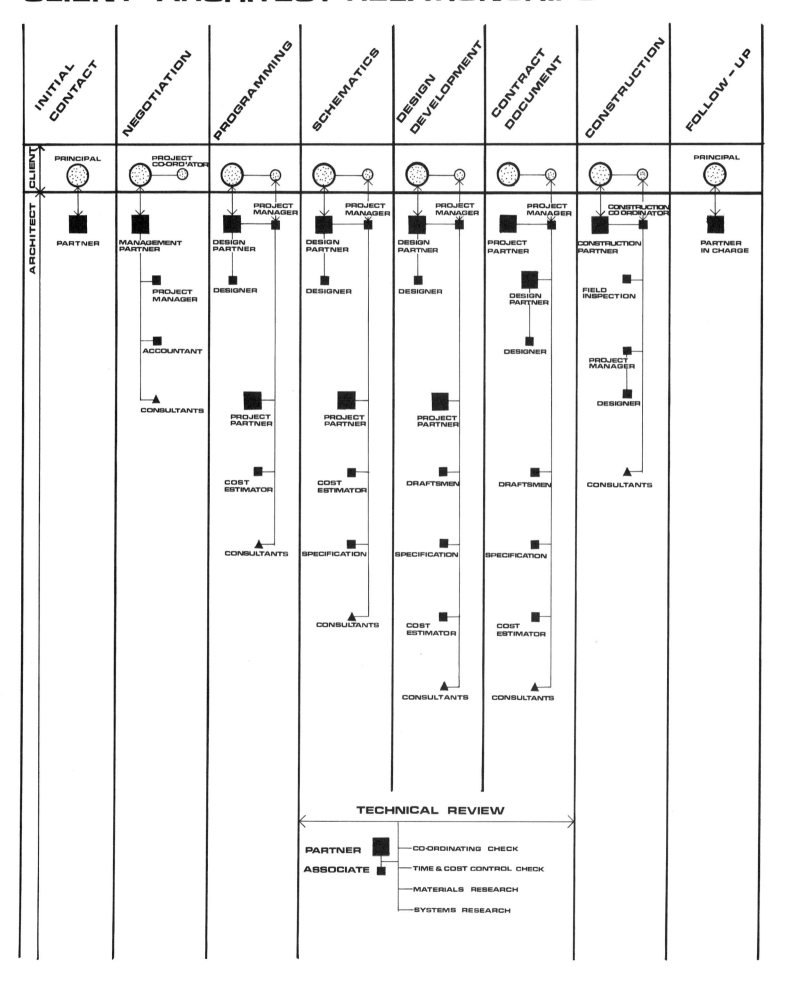

the architect's work vocabulary that merely keeping abreast of these developments is a full-time job in itself. Architects are thus constrained to engage in research, evaluation, cost analysis, and recommendation of materials and methods with the assurance that they will withstand the tests of time, use, and client satisfaction. But the

ORGANIZATION CHART

TOTAL OFFICE FORCE · 112 PERSONS

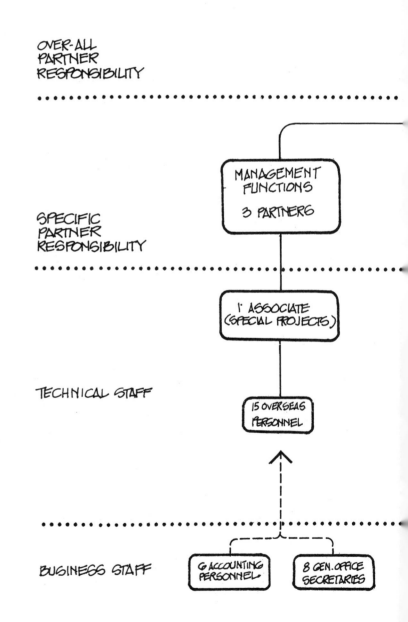

OVER-ALL
PARTNER
RESPONSIBILITY

SPECIFIC
PARTNER
RESPONSIBILITY

MANAGEMENT
FUNCTIONS

3 PARTNERS

1 ASSOCIATE
(SPECIAL PROJECTS)

TECHNICAL STAFF

15 OVERSEAS
PERSONNEL

BUSINESS STAFF

6 ACCOUNTING
PERSONNEL

8 GEN. OFFICE
SECRETARIES

architect's research cannot stop with methods and materials; he can never afford not to know and understand what his colleagues and competitors are doing, technologically and esthetically, in every part of the world. Like the best physicians, engineers, lawyers, and musicians—the best architects never stop learning.

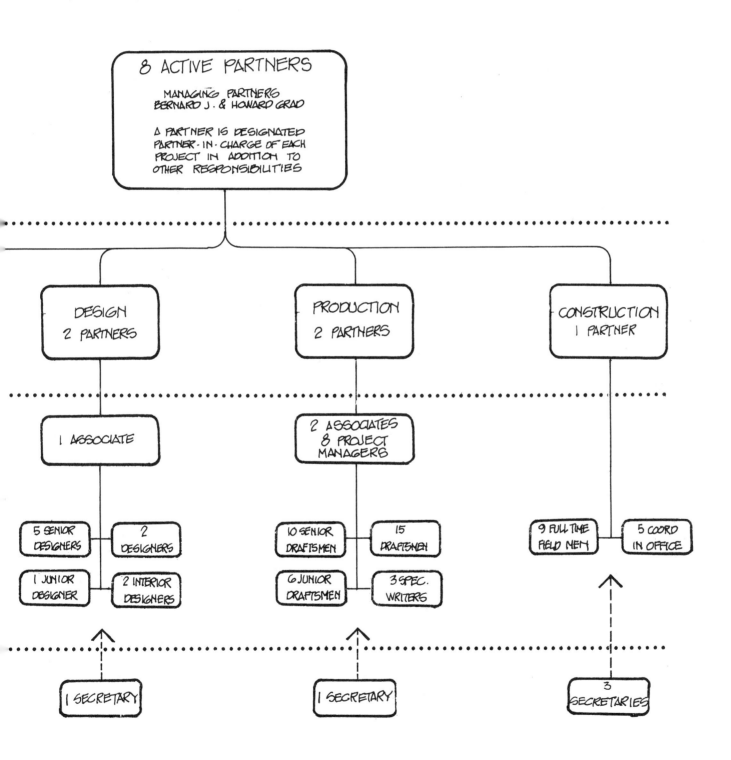

4. *"The Establishment"*

In 1857, architecture was, if not at its nadir, so near as to make no difference. At his best, the architect was not appreciated by the public. At his worst, he was so busy competing with his colleagues and sundry dilettanti that there was even less appreciation within the profession for its own practitioners. The inevitable result was the architectural chaos that still haunts American cities.

In that same abysmal year of 1857, a few architects met in New York in a determined effort to lift their profession by its own bootstraps. This was the inauguration of The American Institute of Architects, which began life by setting itself the frightening task of raising the ethics, the standards, and the level of competence of the profession. How frightening the task was is not difficult to understand: the profession was seething with quarrels over style; there were no schools of architecture; few books on the subject existed, and the young practitioner could find no means of furthering his education.

The founders of the AIA began by systematically interchanging all their technical information and thus creating the nucleus of a body of knowledge that would be available to all comers. Before they could go much farther, the Civil War intervened, and, after its four years, the nation was long beset with the manifold problems of reunification and reconstruction. It was not until 1868 that the AIA's trustees could undertake a personal journey of study through the architectural schools of Europe. This brought about the establishment of the first such school in this country at the Massachusetts Institute of Technology, which opened with an enrollment of four students in 1869. In less than a century, architectural education has grown to include seventy-five schools, of which sixty-three are accredited by the National Architectural Accrediting Board. This body came into being in 1940, largely through the help of the AIA. Now these schools are graduating some twenty-five hundred men and women every year into a profession whose ethical standards and professional conduct are a model to any discipline. Competence is equally emphasized. No graduate can practice until he has passed an examination and received a license from the Architectural Registration Board of his state, and no state lacks such a board.

This is a direct result of the credo that was adopted by the AIA long ago. "The objectives of The American Institute of Architects shall be to organize and unite in fellowship the architects of the United States of America, to combine their efforts so as to promote the esthetic, scientific and practical efficiency of the profession, to advance the science and art of planning and building by advancing the standards of architectural education, training and practice, to co-ordinate the building industry and the profession of architecture, to insure the advancement of the living standards of our people through their improved environment and to make the profession of ever-increasing service to society."

The ways in which the AIA works toward its goals are as numerous as its members. It is not merely a set of attractively symmetrical initials: it is people, professional men and women dedicated to their field. Of course, no organization can automatically imbue its members with professional competence nor guarantee them the public recognition they want: these things each must earn for himself. But in the complexities of modern society, architects can work well only in the climate of high professional standards and ethics and of the public esteem created by himself and his colleagues in the fellowship of the Institute.

Through the AIA's efforts to codify strict standards of competition, to develop standard construction documents, and to regulate the establishment of appropriate fee structures, the young architect enters practice with the firm support of recognized professional practices. Of the thirty thousand architects in the United States today, about twenty thousand are members of the AIA. Membership is open to every practitioner, in this country, its territories, and possessions, who can satisfy his local chapter and the Institute's membership committee that he possesses the necessary qualifications.

At present, the Institute consists of 165 chapters and twenty-four state organizations. Naturally, the scope, direction, and success of each, and of the national institute depends on the active initiative and participation of every member. The cumulative effect of the Institute's work, through its numerous committees, has, in the past one hundred years, produced codes of standards and ethics, professional prestige, and public recognition far in excess of the dreams of its founders. It has evolved, for instance, a national guide and rules governing competitions and client relations, formulas for efficient office practices (how often one hears a professional man, praised for his skill and then damned because "he needs to learn how to run his office"), patterns for contracts and other legal documents, group insurance programs, systems for disseminating technical information, and innumerable other aids that no practitioner can afford to lack.

But all these AIA activities go far beyond the improvement of individual proficiency or professional standing. They are dynamic illustrations of the Institute's resolve "to make the profession of ever-increasing service to society." For the American people, the combined efforts of their architects mean a clear, united drive to build a better environment for all of us. The code, formulated by the Institute, is worth reading word for word.

Approximately fifty AIA committees are occupied with the actualities of public service. Each evolves and recommends policies within its stipulated jurisdiction. These committees are grouped into five commissions which, in turn, co-ordinate the work of the committees and act as liaison with the board of directors.

The Commission on Professional Society embraces the committees dealing with membership, leadership, rules, honors, ethics, and the AIA's physical plant in Washington. This includes disciplinary action for breaches of the standards of ethical practice. Like medicine and law, architecture expects its practitioners to obey a strict code. It is exemplarily just, both substantively and procedurally, in investigating accusations against members. If the charges are proved, disciplinary action is commensurate with the gravity of the offense. This commission's jurisdiction also embraces virtually all the honors bestowed by the Institute—except the highest, its Gold Medal, which is awarded by the directors and they alone may nominate candidates. The AIA's other honors are various, and are conferred on both the man and the work. Local chapter officers are invited to submit nominations for excellence in a number of types of

The Standards of Professional Practice

The following Provisions of the Bylaws of The Institute

form the basis for all disciplinary actions taken under the

Standards of Professional Practice:

CHAPTER 14, ARTICLE 1, SECTION 1 (c)

Any deviation by a corporate member from any of the Standards of Professional Practice of The Institute or from any of the rules of the Board supplemental thereto, or any action by him that is detrimental to the best interests of the profession and The Institute shall be deemed to be unprofessional conduct on his part, and ipso facto he shall be subject to discipline by The Institute.

Preface

0.1 The profession of architecture calls for men of integrity, culture, acumen, creative ability and skill. The services of an architect may include any services appropriate to the development of man's physical environment, provided that the architect maintains his professional integrity and that his services further the ultimate goal of creating an environment of orderliness and beauty. The architect's motives, abilities and conduct always must be such as to command respect and confidence.

An architect should seek opportunities to be of constructive service in civic affairs, and to advance the safety, health, beauty and well-being of his community in which he resides or practices. As an architect, he must recognize that he has moral obligations to society beyond the requirements of law or business practices. He is engaged in a profession which carries important responsibilities to the public and, therefore, in fulfilling the needs of his client, the architect must consider the public interest and the well-being of society.

0.2 An architect's honesty of purpose must be above suspicion; he renders professional services to his client and acts as his client's agent and adviser. His advice to his client must be sound and unprejudiced, as he is charged with the exercise of impartial judgment in interpreting contract documents.

0.3 Every architect should contribute generously of his time and talents to foster justice, courtesy, and sincerity within his profession. He administers and coordinates the efforts of his professional associates, subordinates, and consultants, and his acts must be prudent and knowledgeable.

0.4 Building contractors and their related crafts and skills are obligated to follow the architect's directions as expressed in the contract documents; these directions must be clear, concise, and fair.

THE AMERICAN INSTITUTE OF ARCHITECTS

Obligations

1. To the Public

1.1 An architect may offer his services to anyone on the generally accepted basis of commission, fee, salary, or royalty, as agent, consultant, adviser, or assistant, provided that he strictly maintains his professional integrity.

1.2 An architect shall perform his professional services with competence, and shall properly serve the interests of his client and the public.

1.3 An architect shall not engage in building contracting.

1.4 An architect shall not use paid advertising or indulge in self-laudatory, exaggerated, misleading or false publicity, nor shall he publicly endorse products or permit the use of his name to imply endorsement.

1.5 An architect shall not solicit, nor permit others to solicit in his name, advertisements or other support toward the cost of any publication presenting his work.

1.6 An architect shall conform to the registration laws governing the practice of architecture in any state in which he practices, and shall observe the customs and standards established by the local professional body of architects.

2. To the Client

2.1 An architect's relation to his client is based upon the concept of agency. Before undertaking any commission he shall determine with his client the scope of the project, the nature and extent of the services he will perform and his compensation for them, and shall provide confirmation thereof in writing. In performing his services he shall maintain an understanding with his client regarding the project, its developing solutions and its estimated probable costs. Where a fixed limit of cost is established in advance of design, the architect must determine the character of design construction so as to meet as nearly as feasible the cost limit established. He shall keep his client informed with competent estimates of probable costs. He shall not guarantee the final cost, which will be determined not only by the architect's solution of the owner's requirements, but by the fluctuating conditions of the competitive construction market.

2.2 An architect shall guard the interest of his client and the rights of those whose contracts the architect administers. An architect should give every reasonable aid toward a complete understanding of those contracts in order that mistakes may be avoided.

2.3 An architect's communications, whether oral, written, or graphic, should be definite and clear.

2.4 An architect shall not have financial or personal interests which might tend to compromise his obligation to his client.

2.5 An architect shall not accept any compensation for his professional services from anyone other than his client or employer.

2.6 An architect shall base his compensation on the value of the services he agrees to render. He shall neither offer nor agree to perform his services for a compensation that will tend to jeopardize the adequacy or professional quality of those services, or the judgment, care and diligence necessary properly to discharge his responsibilities to his client and the public.

3. To the Profession

3.1 A member shall support the interests, objectives and Standards of Professional Practice of The American Institute of Architects.

3.2 An architect shall not act in a manner detrimental to the best interests of the profession.

3.3 An architect shall not knowingly injure or attempt to injure falsely or maliciously the professional reputation, prospects, or practice of another architect.

3.4 An architect shall not attempt to supplant another architect after definite steps have been taken by a client toward the latter's employment. He shall not offer to undertake a commission for which he knows another architect has been employed, nor shall he undertake such a commission until he has notified such other architect of the fact in writing, and has been advised by the owner that employment of that architect has been terminated.

3.5 An architect shall not enter into competitive bidding against another architect on the basis of compensation. He shall not use donation or misleading information on cost as a device for obtaining a competitive advantage.

3.6 An architect shall not offer his services in a competition except as provided in the Competition Code of The American Institute of Architects.

3.7 An architect shall not engage a commission agent to solicit work in his behalf.

3.8 An architect shall not call upon a contractor to provide work to remedy omissions or errors in the contract documents without proper compensation to the contractor.

3.9 An architect shall not serve as an employee of unregistered individuals who offer architectural services to the public, nor as an employee of a firm whose architectural practice is not under the identified control of a registered architect.

3.10 An architect shall not be, nor continue to be, a member or employee of any firm which practices in a manner inconsistent with these Standards of Professional Practice.

3.11 Dissemination by an architect, or by any component of The Institute, of information concerning judiciary procedures and penalties, beyond the information published or authorized by The Board or its delegated authority, shall be considered to be detrimental to the best interests of the architectural professional.

4. To Related Professionals

4.1 An architect should provide his professional employees with a desirable working environment and compensate them fairly.

4.2 An architect should contribute to the interchange of technical information and experience between architects, the design profession, and the building industry.

4.3 An architect should respect the interests of consultants and associated professionals in a manner consistent with the applicable provisions of these Standards of Practice.

4.4 An architect should recognize the contribution and the professional stature of the related professionals and should collaborate with them in order to create an optimum physical environment.

4.5 An architect should promote interest in the design professions and facilitate the professional development of those in training. He should encourage a continuing education, for himself and others, in the functions, duties, and responsibilities of the design professions, as well as the technical advancement of the art and science of environmental design.

Promulgation

5.1 These Standards of Professional Practice are promulgated to promote the highest ethical standards for the profession of architecture. Thus the enumeration of particular duties in the Standards should not be construed as a denial of others, equally imperative, though not specifically mentioned. Furthermore, the placement of statements of obligation under any category above shall not be construed as limiting the applicability of such statement to the group named, since some obligations have broad application, and have been positioned as they are only as a matter of convenience and emphasis. The primary purpose of disciplinary action under these Standards of Professional Practice is to protect the public and the profession.

5.2 Since adherence to the principles herein enumerated is the obligation of every member of The American Institute of Architects, any deviation therefrom shall be subject to discipline in proportion to its seriousness.

5.3 The Board of Directors of The American Institute of Architects, or its delegated authority, shall have sole power of interpreting these Standards of Professional Practice and its decisions shall be final subject to the provisions of the Bylaws.

NOTE: This 1965 edition of the Standards of Professional Practice differs from the 1964 edition only in the wording of Paragraph 3.1.

The 1964 edition was a complete revision of the previously existing document.

building design, as well as for achievement in such allied arts as painting and sculpture. In addition, every year a few outstanding architects are advanced to the rank of Fellowship in the Institute. How keenly this is coveted may be inferred from the fact that only 750 of the 20,000 members are Fellows of The American Institute of Architects. The selection procedure is purely democratic: the members of each chapter nominate those of their colleagues who seem to them to merit the honor, and the nominations are submitted to a jury of existing Fellows.

The AIA's Commission on Education includes the committees governing scholastics, training, registration, and research. The Commission on Professional Practice coordinates the committees engaged in standards of architectural practice. The Commission on Architectural Design covers those committees devoted to esthetics and the architectural design of buildings, their facilities, urban design and housing, and their environments. The Commission on Public Affairs comprises the committees dealing with public service, public relations, government and international relations. The fifty-odd committees thus co-ordinated are no mere paper bodies. Their members devote considerable time and energy not only to matters of immediate concern to their profession but to related professions and trades, to technological developments and their implications in future educational changes, to social, political, and economic evolution, and to the preservation of historic and artistic landmarks.

All of this reflects the radical changes in the profession since the chaotic instability of the early 1920's. Not only has the profession matured and sobered but, to a greater degree, so has its environment. The disastrous economic peaks and plunges of the past, that most architectural offices had to expect as inevitable, seem largely to have flattened in the last fifteen years, and if the forecasts of the national future have any validity, there is today a reasonable promise of stabilization.

Commissions

The evolution of society and the profession has led to many other dramatic modifications. One of the most prominent illustrations is the down-to-earth business of getting clients and commissions. In the past, as a rule, there were only two possibilities: choose the right parents or become a joiner. The provident choosers of parents arranged to be born into that circle of wealth, social connections, and eligibility for good clubs that could be relied upon to limit its architectural commissions—residential, industrial, or commercial—to its own members and their friends. The outsiders had to become Elks, Eagles, Tall Cedars, Masons, Moose, Shriners, Pythians, Odd Fellows, or even odder things. When they could, they also joined political organizations where, they hoped, their contacts with public officials would materialize into commissions.

Thirty or forty years ago, when there was no mass media in the sense in which it flourishes today, it was much more difficult for the architect to project himself into any group. The general press paid little, if any, attention to architecture; it was a rare newspaper that had even one reporter interested in the esthetics of the profession. As a result the public knew little and cared less. The architectural press was almost equally limited, and its audience was extremely narrow—it is doubtful whether any architectural magazine had more than a handful of readers outside the profession. Both government and industry were almost totally uninterested.

But today the importance of architects is continually impressed on industry and government officials, as well as the general public, by the exploding population and the formidable amount of construction needed to accommodate them. Burgeoning renewal programs invite architects, large and small, to compete with one another in an ethical, organized fashion. The day of the joiner has ended, to no one's loss. Today most architects engage in actual community services of all kinds that benefit both themselves and their communities.

While the architect, like the doctor and the lawyer, is forbidden to advertise or to engage in gross self-exploitation, legitimate public relations activity, including respectable publicity, is not only permitted but encouraged. Publicity, nowadays, is less elusive for the architect. He and his work are the subject of often unsolicited newspaper stories, magazine articles, features in house organs, and radio and television programs. Architectural publications themselves are being read more and more by laymen as well as by people with tangential interest in the profession. All this exposure means that not only has the awareness of architecture begun to grow but, at least in some circles, the names and work of individual architects have become known.

The AIA and its local chapters conduct a continuing public relations program designed to increase public understanding and appreciation of the profession and its contributions. In addition, it urges the individual architect to ethically utilize the public relations tools in his hand: his services, opinions, civic activities, clients, and his office. These may be employed in speeches, in voluntary public service, in signed articles in general publications, in photographs of his work (not of himself!), in news stories about his projects, in participation in public forums and broadcasts, in cooperation with other professions on matters of common or public interest, and in assisting in the formulation or revision of building codes and zoning laws. Some architects handle their own public relations or designate members of their staffs to specialize in the field; others retain professional public relations counsel. The AIA itself has prepared various pamphlets to guide the architect in an ethical public relations program.

In general, potential clients, both governmental and private, have adopted the interview before a committee as a means of selecting architects. Often an architect hears through friends or business associates that an individual, a partnership, a company, or a government agency is embarking on a construction program. He then puts himself on record with the prospective client by submitting a brochure illustrating and describing his previous work. This, at the same time, automatically refers the prospect to his earlier clients, whose recommendations will usually be invaluable. It is this sort of submission that leads to an invitation to be interviewed, a procedure generally followed by corporations, school boards, and the many agencies of government.

Such sessions are by no means the only way in which an architect approaches clients. In our firm, we prefer, whenever possible, to invite our prospective client to our office so that we can show him the full range of our facilities and let him meet the key people involved in our work. Naturally it is not always feasible for the prospect to come to us, and I suppose we go to him about as often as he accepts our invitation. Because time is a precious commodity, we try to limit the presentation of our qualifications to an hour. The general format of our presentation starts with a brief history of the firm, and outlines the experience of our principals, key personnel, and the numbers of technical people on our staff. This is usually best demonstrated by a graphic table of organization which explains the functions and interactions of an architect's office.

After this brief introduction, attention is then focused upon the particular type of project under consideration. Using color slides, we show examples of work similar to what the client has in mind. This visual display contains a sequence of photographs: an original color rendering of our concept, the scale model of the project, and photos of the finished building.

A prospective client can readily grasp the consistency and accuracy which we strive to achieve so that the final result flows from our original design concept. The verbal and graphic presentation is, in most interviews, followed by a question and answer period during which we are queried on many subjects: time required for design and construction, personnel from our office in charge of the project, and method of daily client contact. Once again, we refer to graphics; charts are used to define our duties and functions and also, the part the client must play for a successful association between both parties.

It is normal for a client to approach a number of architects. Usually three or four and even as many as eight firms are interviewed. In rare cases some public bodies have interviewed many more. The field is then narrowed down and the finalists are called back for further discussion.

Customarily, a few days after the last interview, the client weighs each architect's presentation and makes a decision in favor of the lucky one.

The system of interviewing architects has its amusing aspects in addition to the serious business of preparing and making impressive presentations. On many an occasion we meet our competition, either on our way in or out of an interview—you can imagine the banter that goes back and forth at such an encounter.

Having served as a consultant for several clients, I have had the opportunity to sit on the other side of the table. Listening and watching my colleagues during a presentation is like looking into a mirror. It makes me more than appreciate an experience in the Philadelphia Navy Yard.

Some years ago we were the eighth and last firm to be interviewed by the Navy Contract Board who had spent two full days hearing presentations. They heard four firms each day, two in morning sessions and two each afternoon.

Our firm had done a number of projects for this naval district and we had come to know its personnel through our previous associations. Consequently, I knew the chairman of the board who was nice enough to welcome us warmly to our interview.

He appeared harried and exhausted after listening to the same pitch for two days. I wondered how receptive he and his board would be to this final interview.

As we walked into the conference room, I assured him that since our firm and its experience was well known to the board, we would make our presentation brief. Thanking me, he then made this observation: "Bernie," he said, "I've sat through so many of these presentations that I can tell by an architect's looks what sort of a pitch he will make. Over the years I've categorized architects into the following types: First, we have the pipe smoker in sport jacket and odd slacks; next, there is the conservative dresser with crew cut and horn-rimmed glasses; then, the Madison Avenue huckster with his six-pointed handkerchief in the breast pocket of his English-cut suit, and finally, the bow tie specialist. Each type has a particular approach and I guarantee that I can spot what he will say by the clothes he wears."

Fees

As a prelude to any discussion of fees, it should be clearly understood that architects do not win commissions by competing with each other on a fee basis. Architects are selected on the basis of qualifications, ability, and experience.

In rare cases a group of architects may be invited to enter into a formal competition conducted under conditions recommended by the AIA. Under these auspices each competitor is paid for his competitive efforts and the winner is awarded the commission.

Sometime in the pre-history of the profession, an anonymous maker of traditions set up the magic figure of six percent of the building's cost as the minimum fee that an architect should charge. For generations that figure has been basic, despite all the changes in the economic, social, and political structure of our country. For the past decade most chapters of the AIA have been trying, with some success, to revise the fee system to correspond with the effort expended by the architect on the project in question.

This duplication of the Schedule of Recommended Minimum Fees of the New Jersey Chapter of the AIA explains in detail the fees which are applicable to the various categories of construction. It will be quickly noted that the lower percentages apply to simpler projects and the higher fees are geared to more complex works. At a glance it can be seen that the larger the dollar value of the work, the less the percentage of fee.

Categorizing the types of construction has helped to remove the inequities of the rigid fixed-percentage fee system, and a good illustration is to compare the work entailed in a million dollar garage with that of designing a million dollar laboratory.

Certainly the time and thought demanded by the complicated facilities of a laboratory far exceed what is needed to design a garage. But, under the rigid percentage system, the same fee would have been paid for each, despite the gross disparities involved.

It would be fair to say that the method of categorizing types of construction is a logical method of establishing fees on the percentage basis.

Two other methods of fee compensation have been developed and are part of most of the fee schedules recommended throughout the United States:

1. The conversion of a percentage fee to a lump sum when the scope of the project has become clearly defined. This enables both owner and architect to enter into an agreement for a fixed price for architectural and engineering services.

2. In many instances the scope of a project is not clearly defined at the outset, and it becomes necessary for both owner and architect to engage in research. Then the system of paying the architect on a time-factor basis has proved to be an equitable arrangement. This system simply means that, in addition to the architect's direct payroll costs, he is further compensated for his overhead and profit by adding a factor to his direct payroll. Arithmetically, this means that for every dollar he spends in direct payroll, he will receive between one and one-half and two dollars for overhead and profit.

One of the major obstacles to the development of a system of fees consonant with the complexity of the work, however, is what one might call the "assembly line" architects who turn out repetitive, template designs for houses, apartment buildings, speculative office buildings, schools, shopping centers and so on. Because their volume permits them to run off these designs at cut-rates, they fear personal harm from any recommended fee structure. Unfortunately, they are flattering their clients' as well as their own blind spots, especially in the case of uninformed public officials who believe that price alone determines what is a good buy. These men pay for stale architecture and they get it. They and the mass builders who patronize the discount architect attempt to argue that since construction costs are always going up, the architect's percentage rises

SCHEDULE OF RECOMMENDED MINIMUM FEES

Cost of the work in dollars

Category Number	50,000	100,000	250,000	500,000	750,000	1 Million	5 Million	10 Million
1	7	6.5	6	5.5	5.25	5	4.5	4
2	8	7.5	7	6.5	6.25	6	5.5	5
3	9	8.5	8	7.5	7.25	7	6.5	5.75
4	10	9	8.5	8	7.75	7.5	6.75	6
5	11	10	9	8.5	8.25	8	7.5	7
6	12	11	10	9.5	9	8.5	8	7.5
7	12.5	11.5	11	10	10	10	10	10
8	15	15	14	13	12	11	9	8.5

BUILDING TYPE	CATEGORY NUMBER
Administration Building	4
Airport Hangar	2
Airport Terminal	3
Alterations & Additions (Note 6)	
Apartment Hotel	2
Apartment House (Note 9)	2
Armory	3
Art Gallery	6
Asylum-Sanitorium	5
Automobile & Service Facility	2
Band Shell	5
Bank	5
Church or Chapel	6
Clinic	5
Club — Civic, Fraternal, Country	5
College or University (Notes 4 & 8)	
College Building — w/o Special Facilities	4
College Building — with Special Facilities	5
Communications Building	5
Community Building	4
Concert Hall	6
Convent	3
Convention Hall	3
Correction Building — Housing Area	3
Correction Building — Program Area	4
Department Store	4
Dormitory	4
Emergency Squad Station	3
Exchange	5
Exposition Building	3
Fire Station	3
Fixtures & Equipment (Note 10)	8
Funeral Building	6
Furniture & Furnishings (Note 10)	8
Garage	1
Home for Aged (Non-Convalescent or Remedial)	3
Hotel — Transient	3
Hospital (Notes 4 & 8)	5
Housing (see Apartment)	
Industrial Building	1
Industrial Building — Special Occupancy	2
Interiors & Displays (Note 10)	8

BUILDING TYPE	CATEGORY NUMBER
Laboratory	5
Library	4
Loft Building	1
Long Term Care — Medical	5
Long Term Care — Residential	4
Market — Public	2
Medical Health Center	5
Medical or Dental Office Building	3
Memorials	8
Monastery	3
Motel	3
Municipal Building	4
Museum	6
Nursing Home — Convalescent	4
Nursing Home — Remedial	5
Office Building — Commercial & Rental	2
Office Building — Special Occupancy	3
Plant — Printing or Processing	2
Playground	5
Police Station	3
Public Buildings — Monumental	6
Race Track	3
Recreation or Park Building	5
Research & Data Center	5
Residence — Development Type (Note 9)	2
Residence — Individual	7
Restorations	8
Restaurant	5
School — Private	4
School — Public	3
Shopping Center (Note 8)	3
Shops & Stores — Retail	3
Special Structures & Buildings	8
Stadium	3
Station — Bus & Rail	3
Swimming Pool	5
Synagogue or Temple	6
Theater — Cinema	3
Theater — Legitimate	6
University (see College)	
Utilitarian Structure	1
Warehouse	1

BUILDING TYPE CATEGORIES

1. Garage; Industrial Building; Loft Building; Utilitarian Structure; Warehouse.

2. Airport Hangar; Apartment Hotel; Apartment House (Note 9); Automobile & Service Facility; Industrial Building — Special Occupancy; Market — Public; Office Building — Commercial and Rental; Plant — Printing or Processing; Residence — Development Type (Note 9).

3. Airport Terminal; Armory; Convent; Convention Hall; Correction Building — Housing Area; Emergency Squad Station; Exposition Building; Fire Station; Home for Aged (non-Convalescent or Remedial); Hotel — Transient; Medical or Dental Office Building; Monastery; Motel; Office Building — Special Occupancy; Police Station; Race Track; School — Public; Shopping Center (Note 8); Shops and Stores — Retail; Stadium; Station — Bus & Rail; Theater — Cinema.

4. Administration Building; College Building — without Special Facilities; Community Building; Correction Building — Program Area; Department Store; Dormitory; Library; Long Term Care — Residential; Municipal Building; School — Private.

5. Band Shell; Bank; Clinic; Club — Civic, Fraternal, Country; College Building — with Special Facilities; Communications Building; Exchange; Hospital (Notes 4 and 8); Laboratory; Long Term Care — Medical; Medical Health Center; Playground; Recreation or Park Building; Research & Data Center; Restaurant; Swimming Pool.

6. Art Gallery; Church or Chapel; Concert Hall; Funeral Building; Museum; Public Buildings — Monumental; Synagogue or Temple; Theater — Legitimate.

7. Residence — Individual.

8. Fixtures & Equipment (Note 10); Furniture & Furnishings (Note 10); Interiors and Displays (Note 10); Memorials; Restorations; Special Structures and Buildings.

GENERAL NOTES

1. This Fee Schedule is applicable to Owner-Architect Agreement on a Percentage Basis Including Engineering Services (AIA Document B-131), for work let on a single lump sum construction contract. The percentage is based on the cost of the work, and the services include normal engineering.

Other methods may be employed as follows: Professional Fee plus Expense (AIA Document B-311), Multiple of Direct Personnel Expense (AIA Document B-211), Per Diem or Hourly Rate. Certain types of projects, special conditions of practice or individual preference may indicate that the Architect's fee can be determined more equitably by one of these alternate methods.

Personal services of the Architect for consultation, or for testifying in a law suit or arbitration proceedings, provided he is not one of the parties involved, should be performed on a per diem basis, established by negotiation, plus travel and living expenses if any are required.

When the Architect is engaged for limited services, applicable tabular fee rates may be adjusted.

2. As the dollar magnitude of project construction cost increases, economies in cost of architectural services are reflected in the lower fees scheduled. These vary with project type, but higher fees than those in the schedule are reasonable for unusual character of structure, complex electrical or mechanical facilities, or other special requirements.

When project construction costs exceed ten million dollars, the fee is subject to individual negotiation because of the variables in a project of this magnitude.

3. When project construction cost falls between the tabular limits, basic fees are determined by interpolation.

Fees for building types not listed in the building type index should be determined by the fees indicated for structures of similar design complexity.

4. When a project includes several types of structures, the scheduled fees apply to such types individually.

5. When charges for services are based on a Multiple of Direct Personnel Expense, such expense is defined as the aggregate of net time card costs plus normal benefits. The multiple factor to be used to establish the Architect's compensation and to cover his overhead costs is subject to negotiation. The recommended minimum for such multiple factor is $2\frac{1}{2}$ times the Direct Personnel Expense.

6. Alterations to structures involve conditions that complicate and extend the normal basic professional services. Basic fees for altered structures in all categories are recommended to be increased by 4%.

Additions to existing buildings also imply more extended architectural services. It is recommended that the Owner and Architect agree on a fee which is between the basic fee and the fee for alterations and which recognizes the proper degree of additional services required.

7. Construction work let on a cost plus fee basis, or work let under separate lump sum contracts requires service over and above the basic services and additional charges should be agreed upon before any such service is performed.

8. Master planning, feasibility studies, program development, site planning, and work of a similar nature should be performed on a basis of a Multiple of Direct Personnel Expense, or on a basis of a Professional Fee plus Expense.

9. Repetitive elements in a project influence the fee structure. The following building types are examples: Apartment House; Residence — Development Type. Fees may be applied to total cost of project or to initial basic designs and negotiated for duplication of elements. The fee for site planning and site development should be established as recommended in No. 8.

10. Interior decoration and design of furniture, furnishings, displays, and special equipment should be performed on a basis of a Multiple of Direct Personnel Expense, or Fee Schedule No. 8 when the volume of work warrants the application of a percentage basis.

enough in dollar terms to compensate him for his more complex endeavors. Not only is this not even plausible, it just ain't so!

Though a surgeon may legitimately charge more for a lung section than for a tonsillectomy, an architect must accept the same percentage fee regardless of the amount of his time that is required for his project. The architect, like the surgeon, finds his basic costs of doing business much higher than they were in earlier periods. It is worthwhile examining them because they, too, reflect the changes that have taken place both in the profession and in the society in which it functions.

Primarily, there is the fact that architecture today entails many more services than was traditionally the case. An almost equally important factor in the increased costs of running an office, architectural or otherwise, is the previously unknown and now inescapable payroll-collateral overhead: social security contributions, unemployment insurance taxes, paid sick leave, more holidays and vacations, employee hospitalization premiums, and bonus plans. Today's architect carries more insurance than his predecessors ever did for such contingencies as disability incurred on the job by field representatives and life insurance on key employees who must travel by air.

Changes in jurisprudence have exposed the architect for the first time to the grave hazard known as errors and omissions, and the burden of defending such third-party actions. Because of this vulnerability most firms, for their own protection, are burdened with high insurance premiums.

Obviously, then, the architect works in no ivory tower, immune to the customary costs of doing business. Like his clients, he needs an office, people, and facilities; like the rest of the world, he has to pay the going price for these necessities.

Payments

The architect is normally paid for his services on this percentage of completion:

Schematic Design Phase	15%
Design Development Phase	20%
Construction Documents Phase	40%
Construction Phase	25%

I am certain that there will arise in the minds of many readers the question of profit. Just how much profit is there in the practice of architecture?

An indication of changing times is dramatically demonstrated by a survey recently commissioned by the American Institute of Architects. This study, in which 223 offices participated, represented a cross-section of the profession and revealed that the profit chase is an elusive one for the architect if he does not pay heed to the business sector of his work. Two startling facts were revealed:

1. Changes in economics show that from 1950 to 1966 the pre-tax income or profit factor has decreased from 20 percent to an average of 10 percent of the gross fee.

2. That architects must be able to design profits as well as buildings!

For those who are interested in detail there follows a budget of an architect's fee, divided into its basic components.

BUDGET BREAKDOWN AND DISTRIBUTION OF THE ARCHITECT'S FEE

In order to understand the percentages and allocations of the fee to the various phases of an architect's effort, these facts are recognized as accepted practices within the profession:

1. A pre-tax profit, equal to approximately 20 percent of the total fee, is the sum most architects expect to realize for their services.

2. For every dollar spent on direct, technical payroll, it costs the architect another dollar in indirect expenses to stay in business. These are the items which the term indirect expenses embraces:

Rent
Drafting supplies
Specifications printing
Photos
Renderings
Telephone and telegrams
Insurance
Office expenses
Personnel ads
Stationery and postage
Legal and audit fees
Computer time rental
Bank charges and interest

Contributions
Fringe benefits
Brochures
Personal property taxes
Social Security taxes
State Unemployment taxes
Federal Unemployment insurance
Partners' salaries
Auto rental and expenses
Office equipment leasing
Public relations expenses

3. Direct expenses are those that are attributable to a specific project as compared to the indirect expenses which pertain to all projects executed in a given year.

4. Consultants' fees are generally in accordance with these accepted norms:

Structural engineering. Between one-half of one percent and one percent of the total cost of the project;

Heating, ventilating, plumbing and electrical engineering. Approximately three-quarters of the architect's fee as it relates to the cost of the heating, ventilating, plumbing, and electrical work in the project;

Other consultants. Fees are negotiated in accordance with the effort involved.

The weakness of the percentage system is best shown by what happened to us a few years ago in designing a regional office building for The Prudential Insurance Company. While we were developing this 225,000 square foot building, the Prudential decided to increase its area and add some features not included in the original program. Initially, we had agreed on a cost of twenty-three dollars per square foot, and a five million dollar budget had been established. The revisions of the program made it necessary for me to confer with Prudential's officers. Here I should like to pay tribute to the exemplary understanding displayed by the company in the person of S. Westcott Toole, Vice President in charge of home office real estate. He was responsible for the additions to the original program, and forthwith he increased the budget to conform.

I breathed more easily. We finished our drawings and specifications and sent them out for bids by six selected firms. The low bid—though all were very close—was one million dollars below our estimate. The job had hit the market when work was scarce and

FRANK GRAD & SONS
Architects-Engineers

PROJECT BUDGET
Project No. 1234
XYZ CORPORATION

Budget No. 2
Date   20 APRIL 1965

1. ESTIMATED FEE:
   Basic: 7 % x $1,000,000 = $70,000
   Extras: = _____
                                     $70,000   (100%)

2. FEES TO CONSULTANTS:
   Struct.   .7 % x 1,000,000 =   7,000
   M. & E. ¾ of   7 % x   350,000 = 18,375
   Kit. none   % x   =
   Land. lump
      sum   % x   =   1,125
   Costs none   =   1,500
   Other   = _____
                                       $28,000   (40%)

3. AVAILABLE TO GRAD (1–2) $42,000

4. ESTIMATED PROFIT = 14,000   (20%)

5. ESTIMATED DIRECT
   EXPENSES   =   1,500   (2%)

6. AVAILABLE FOR OVERHEAD &
   DIRECT PAYROLL (3–5) $26,000

7. ALLOWANCE FOR OVERHEAD $13,000   (19%)

8. AVAILABLE FOR DIRECT
   PAYROLL (6–7) $13,000   (19%)

DIRECT PAYROLL BREAKDOWN

SCHEMATIC DESIGN	15%	$ 1,950
DESIGN DEVELOPMENT	20%	2,600
CONSTR. DOCUMENTS	40%	5,200
CONSTRUCTION ADMIN.	25%	3,250
	100%	$13,000

prices were low. All to the good for the client, but what about the architect? Sixty thousand dollars in percentage had gone flying out the window! Of course, we built up a great deal of valuable good will with the client, but at the time we did not relish the financial blow. This, however, is an unusual instance. We are always pleased when the bids fall short of our estimate, but in this case the illustration is ideal in showing the weakness of the percentage system.

Nowadays, on the other hand, many clients insist on a clause in the architect's contract to make him answerable for redesign if his project exceeds the budget. This one-way street is not an equitable arrangement.

When a client questions the fee basis, one of the most difficult points to explain to his satisfaction is that, for every dollar spent on direct technical payroll, the architect must spend another dollar for overhead components. This is in addition to those of the normal office, such as rent, heat, light, supplies, and so on. The expenses built into today's architectural practice include public relations, accountancy and legal counsel, brochures, travel, study and research—which includes sending key personnel to seminars in distant places—and the amount of time that is given, without charge, to public service. This is why architects want their fee schedule to be established on a solid basis not only equitable to them but to their clients. Such an achievement will help to attract to the profession many young people who are admirably endowed for architecture but who are understandably concerned with the monetary return on their time and talent.

Architecture differs from other professions in that the relationship with the client is inanimate, almost impersonal. The doctor, the dentist, the lawyer, even the tax consultant advises and treats patients or clients on a personal and, even, an emotional level. This fact is reflected in the fees that they can command, which are not often measurable in terms of a percentage of anything. But even when an architect's client knows that a new building will double his profits, he often tries to bargain down the fee as far as he can; at the same time he is spending millions advertising the products that will be made or marketed in his new building.

Time is another difficult element when one is discussing money with a client. No architect wants to dally over a job, one reason being that he has to complete it before he can move on to the next. But with the normal human addiction to procrastination, most people and companies—which are composed of people—seem to spend an inordinate amount of time in hatching construction projects.

Then, when the egg has broken, they expect designs to be worked out and buildings to be erected virtually overnight. Clients should recognize that realization takes time; it would cost them no more in money, and far less in time, if they would call in architectural counsel at the inception of anticipated construction plans.

Joint Ventures

The spectacular growth of the construction industry was initiated by the needs of the Second World War. As a result, the two or even five million dollar project has been robbed of its former dazzle by the almost everyday occurrence of building programs costing ten to twenty times as much. Such costly and complex projects are responsible for the revolutionary introduction of the joint venture into architectural practice. The joint venture was a natural outgrowth of large-scale military projects so vast and so numerous that construction firms had to be brought together to carry them out. From this it was a logical progression to envisage similar temporary marriages of architectural and engineering firms in order to pool their resources and finish a given job in less than the usual time. In the beginning more than one of these marriages was celebrated only because some government agency was holding a shotgun, but they swiftly became a normal means of undertaking large enterprises.

Now architects and engineers who want to work on such projects, either at home or abroad, frequently seek such commissions jointly; in other instances, two or more architectural offices will themselves form such a joint venture. In addition to the obvious advantage of the division of a large load among the many resources of two or more architectural firms, the architect/engineer joint venture (for sometimes these ad hoc marriages grow quite polygamous) affords to all concerned—including the client—the advantages of having all architectural and engineering services under one figurative roof. At the same time, no one is subjected to any of the long-term disadvantages of what might otherwise become an unwieldy and uneconomical agglomeration. Some projects are so huge and of such duration that it becomes expeditious to execute them in a new, separate office rather than in the home offices of any of the participants. Thus the key people are provided by both the architects and the engineers involved, to work together simultaneously and, when necessary, to augment their talents by retaining outside consultants.

5. The Face of Construction

The architect, in a sense, must always serve two masters and, at the same time, interpret each to the other and then arbitrate between them. He is, of course, the agent of the owner who retains him and pays his fee. But his obligation to the owner is matched by his duty to the contractor, whose bid he has joined in approving. If he assumes the role of autocrat toward the contractor, his position will at once become untenable. The sensible architect always strives for a relationship with the contractor that will assure a harmonious operation throughout the construction period.

The architect normally spends up to a year with his client in the development of the documents which represent the project in graphic and verbal form.

The completion of this phase concludes the imaginative and creative aspects of his work and results in a set of working drawings and contract specifications. These are the instruments which the contractor will use in pricing the cost of the project and from which the building will be constructed.

For the next year or two, depending on the size of the project, the architect will maintain a close association not only with his client but with the contractors. It is during this period that he is called upon for his other skills in managing, expediting, interpreting the intent of the drawings and specifications, and arbitrating differences between the various subcontractors.

While work is under way, the architect, on behalf of the owner, must make certain that the architectural drawings and specifications are being followed and that the contractor gives the owner the materials and workmanship he has promised. The architect's right to condemn the contractor's work for deficiencies or inaccuracies is coupled with the power to either certify or disallow the contractor's requests for payment from the owner.

Obviously, the architect is obligated to make everything clear to the contractor in advance. The general conditions of the specifications request the contractor to cooperate in setting up certain procedures in order to expedite the orderly progress of the project. It is usual for the architect to specify the time allotted for the construction operation. The contractor, as one of his first actions on a project, submits a progress schedule so that everyone will know the amount of time to be taken by each of his own or his subcontractor's operations. Very often this is decided by the critical path method: a computerized system of setting up a job schedule by outlining the critical succession of the tasks involved and assigning a time value to each.

The contractor is also asked to submit an itemized cost account of the various trades to be employed. This gives the architect a standard by which to measure each month's accomplishment and thus, approve, question, or disallow the contractor's payment requisitions. The contractor is then supplied with a system for the prompt approval of subcontractors, specified materials, and shop drawings. Agreement is made on how and when his requisitions for payment are to be presented. Finally, a schedule of periodic meetings at the job site is established where representatives of the owner, the architect, the contractor, and his major subcontractors will confer regularly in order to maintain job co-ordination and schedule.

It is not humanly possible to delineate in the working drawings or in the contract specifications every minute procedure entailed in the construction of a building. Many of these are and must be implied. It is easily conceivable that, for one operation, there may be ten possible methods. In this area of methodology the contractor has the right to make his own choice. Here the architect must exercise the utmost discretion, for he never has the right to tell the contractor how to do the job. The courts are full of cases where the architect in the field has dictated method to the contractor and it turns out to have been wrong.

In simpler days, there was an unspoken three-sided assumption of equal responsibility between owner, architect, and contractor and, very possibly, of a moral obligation. Many large buildings were admirably erected on the basis of very simple drawings and specifications. Owners felt responsible to both architects and contractors; architects recognized their obligations toward owners and contractors; and contractors felt their loyalties to owners and architects alike. Each party respected the expertise of the others; all three knew their joint goal, despite the sparse documentation of the time. Now, each of the parties is exposed to so many hazards that he encloses himself within voluminous paper lines of defense. That is why architectural documents today are so vast and so meticulously detailed. At the same time, for his own protection, the contractor often employs lawyers and other specialists to write even his letters of reply to architect's instructions.

And so the profession finds itself once more enmeshed in committees even in the matter of putting up the building after all the plans have been approved. Apparently the era of head-to-head relationships, in which understandings, whether oral or written, are clearly comprehended, has been definitively abolished by the age of the chain of command. But, no matter how many links the chain acquires, the basic principles of the relation between the architect and the construction industry seem indestructibly to survive. The work of an industry whose annual volume exceeds billions is monitored by ten thousand architectural offices employing some number less than the nation's 30,000 architects.

Building is an extremely competitive industry, and, in theory, all one needs, if one wishes to enter it, is the desire and the capital. There are no governing regulations; no authority issues licenses to practice. Theory aside, however, most of the competent contracting firms doing business today are made up of men who have had excellent formal schooling. Many are qualified engineers who have chosen, for diverse reasons, to move into construction, and most contracting staffs are largely directed by engineers.

What is embraced by contracting is, in reality, sixteen separate divisions:

1. General requirements
2. Site work
3. Concrete
4. Masonry
5. Metals
6. Carpentry
7. Moisture protection
8. Doors, windows, and glass
9. Finishes
10. Specialties
11. Equipment
12. Furnishings
13. Special construction
14. Conveying systems
15. Mechanical
16. Electrical

The average contractor, whether large, medium-sized or small, never undertakes all or even most of these trades. He is, in actuality, a business-management expert, a broker, or a purchasing agent. He uses his own field work force on only a minor portion of the total job —perhaps 15 to 20 percent at most, for the concrete, masonry, and carpentry portions—and engages subcontractors for all the rest. When a prime contractor is invited to bid on a job, his ultimate goal is to put together a competitive price that will be lower than any others and still yield a profit. In order to arrive at this price, his own estimators will appraise the material and labor entailed in those trades in which he himself will actively engage; for each of the others, he will invite competitive bids from a number of subcontractors. The preparation of the final estimate by the prime contractor is further complicated in that many manufacturers or vendors will only supply materials, not labor. They submit their prices to the various subcontractors, who must then estimate their own labor separately.

Basically, there are two categories of construction projects: the first is public work, which by law must be assigned on the basis of competitive bidding, since public funds are involved; and second, projects for individuals or corporations. Public work is governed by laws which detail the procedures of public advertising for bids, qualifications of bidders, the place and time of receipt of sealed bids, and the awarding of contracts to the low bidders. Private work is usually bid by a selected list of contractors. From these two fundamental methods, other variations develop. On public works some agencies of the government operate under the principle of the general contract. This means that the total construction operation is the responsibility of the general contractor. In some states there are statutes which provide that the work be assigned on a multiple contract basis. This method divides a project into five or more separate prime contracts: a general contract; structural steel; plumbing; heating, ventilating and air conditioning; and electrical. Other components of the work, such as elevators, kitchen equipment, and movable office partitions, may be separated from the general contract as the governing agency may direct.

The great period of national economic expansion naturally included the construction industry, and a number of interesting developments occurred. These, as in most other industries, were marred by certain excesses and by the inequities that plagued the smaller firms. This was especially true during the Depression and in the first years of massive government engagement in construction. The stagnation of building in the Depression forced most contracting firms to reduce their staffs to minimal skeleton status, retaining only a handful of key people. When it became known, as it easily did, that a government project was planned, the contractors knew at once just how much money had been appropriated for it and could guess quite accurately the figure that would be the winning bid. Each would determine the lowest possible sum at which he could afford to do the job; then he would call for bids from subcontractors, which he would ruthlessly beat down until they fell within his maximum. If the subcontractors were reduced to bankruptcy, it did not distress the prime contractors.

Consequently, when the construction industry began to share in the general economic recovery, some of the higher ranking subcontractors—such as those in the plumbing, heating, structural steel, and electrical trades—formed trade associations designed to aid them in attaining prime contractor rank. Strongly aided by the growing labor lobbies, they succeeded in obtaining federal and often state legislation that required all public construction to be divided into the five basic prime contracting categories: general construction; heating, ventilating and air conditioning; electrical; plumbing; and structural steel. While in private work the owner and architect continued to deal only with a prime general contractor, government projects simply quintupled the architect's prime contractor problems. Subsequently, the federal government and many of the states repealed this kind of law, but far too many states still retain it despite the fact that most architects hold the opinion that it increases construction costs by as much as 15 percent.

A variation in the sector of private work is the negotiated contract. Instead of bidding by a group of contractors, this permits an owner to select a prime contractor and, through negotiation, arrive at an agreeable contractual arrangement. There are several reasons for this type of contract. The owner may wish to save time or there may be a history of previous satisfactory relationship between owner and contractor.

Working under a negotiated contract, the contractor is usually paid a *fixed fee* which represents his profit. Normal competition is still maintained by reason of bidding by all subcontractors. In many cases, the negotiated price agreed to by both parties is, in fact, *a ceiling price*. Both owner and contractor agree to share any savings that result if the final cost is below this ceiling price.

The construction industry today is faced with many problems. The competition is almost fierce. Both general and subcontractors work for a very small margin of profit. More than most industries, they have exaggerated peaks and valleys in their volume of business. Labor, which accounts for about 60 percent of the cost of a building, obviously plays the most important role in determining the final price of a project. The industry is plagued by strikes and jurisdictional disputes. This internal struggle between management and labor cannot help but contribute to the ever-increasing cost of construction.

A troublesome practice is the ban against the architect's specifying any proprietary, non-competitive material or construction method in public projects, though in private work he is free to insist on whatever the owner demands or he himself deems best suited. But every public contract requires the architect to specify at least three manufacturers of every item that goes into the building, and to expand the contractor's choice further by adding, after the three names, "or approved equal." This little phrase is undoubtedly the most dangerous ingredient in today's construction economy, which is so largely dependent on government work.

Even when both the architect and the governmental entity commissioning the project agree most definitely on standards of quality, "or approved equal" in the specifications can impose a wholly unanticipated result. Virtually every product is available in a variety of brands, and each manufacturer will insist that his product is the equal of all the others because it meets the requirements of the United States Bureau of Standards. But very often it satisfies only the minimum set forth in those requirements, whereas what is wanted is the best in the field. Mistakenly, some private clients insist on inserting "or approved equal" into their contracts in the illusion that they are enhancing the competitive spirit of the various contractors and suppliers and will, therefore, get the job done more cheaply. If the criterion is quality, they are right. That is the only thing that will be cheapened because in hard practice "or approved equal" is never equal. The presence of that phrase in any contract is an unmistakable danger signal to the experienced architect.

One of our private clients had commissioned us to design a bonded warehouse and had let the contract on a competitive bid, complete with "or approved equal." The successful bidder was a contractor whom we knew and with whom we had often worked pleasantly in the past. But on this job everything went behind schedule and defects multiplied into disaster. Each weekly job meeting was a crisis. We were sympathetic to the fact that the contractor's profit margin was narrow. We knew his field superintendent was a rather weak individual who was obviously under instructions to save his own firm every possible nickel. Everyone was unhappy, and our office was the unhappiest, because the client was not getting what he should have. We were losing money because of the excessive amount of time that was being spent by our office.

One morning the president of the contracting firm asked me to spend the day with him at the job so that we could resolve all our problems. As he was driving me out to the project, I asked, "Al, why do you fellows think all architects must be two-headed idiots? We spent six to eight months designing this job, we wrote three or four hundred pages of specifications, we spent all this time delineating quality, we gave you three or four choices on each item and yet you haven't submitted one single material that we specified. Everyone has been 'or approved equal,' and therein lies the cause for all the trouble on this job."

"You know," he said as he drove, "You're dumber than I thought. Don't you realize that if we bid this job the way you specified it, we wouldn't have it and we wouldn't be sitting here together?"

Nothing could better illustrate how far, in this nation of paper movers, the construction of a building has departed from the old three-party agreement among owner, architect, and contractor. Then the owner knew what he wanted for his money, the architect designed accordingly, and the contractor accepted not only a legal but a moral obligation to deliver the quality intended. But today, even though we may use a selected list of bidders, everyone of whom we believe to be reputable, the contractors sometimes buy subcontractors so cheaply that the latter have no reasonable margin of profit unless they start scrimping and cutting corners. To say that this complicates the dual obligation of the architect to the owner and the contractor, is hardly to over-state the situation. Too often the owner does not get what he wants and pays for since the contractor and the subcontractor do not give him the saving they have made on the "or approved equal." The architect must constantly fight to preserve some semblance of the quality originally specified, and the contractor can never stop bickering to keep his head above water.

When an architect designs a multi-million dollar structure and opens the market for bids, literally thousands of people are involved until the job is completed. The architect, the engineer, the contractor, the subcontractors, the manufacturers, the vendors, the mechanics, and the workmen must always reckon with the inevitable human errors inherent in co-ordinating the myriad components of the building and the bewildering array of possible methodologies. Yet the owner automatically assumes that on the day he gets the key, his entire work force can move in, pull switches, press buttons, turn knobs, and expect this product of so many thousand minds and hands to function like a watch.

An enlightening and interesting observation is the comparison between the design and construction of buildings and other facilities that the public uses. No ship, automobile, or plane is ever put to use without pilot models, shakedown cruises, test runs, or experimental models. Yet a complicated, man-made building is simply finished and prepared for use immediately.

Owners might well ponder this inconsistency in their expectations and working relationship with architects, engineers, and builders.

6. The Language of Vision

The architect's vocabulary extends far beyond the special words of his profession and its allied fields. In fact, vocabulary, in the architectural sense, is at least as much non-verbal as verbal. It is the sum of the architect's talents, knowledge, education, interests, and individual style.

This vocabulary grows in four steps. The first is his innate affinity, based on his endowments and his fundamental drive, with the verbal and other tools of his profession. His preliminary, classical education is the second step; now he studies man and his history, the development of religion, ethics, government, economics, philosophy, the plastic arts, literature—all the humanities and sciences that enhance his own basic vocabulary and so strongly influence the vocabulary of his profession. The third step, his concentrated architectural study, broadens the foundation of his technical architectural vocabulary and provides the solid base for its enrichment. Finally, his professional career compels never-ending study, research, and exposure to the allied arts and sciences; these factors, augmented by his own avocational interests, virtually guarantee the lifelong expansion of his architectural vocabulary.

Because the simple life has been irretrievably lost and because tomorrow's society will be even more complex than today's, the architect's vocabulary must expand to include the abundance of new techniques, new methods, new materials, and new forms that are being discovered daily. The practice of architecture is far more than the mere disposition of space. To admit ignorance of the engineering components of construction or to acknowledge disinter-

WHITNEY MUSEUM OF AMERICAN ART. Breuer's usual bold concept. Architect: Marcel Breuer and Hamilton Smith. *Photo by Ezra Stoller*

est in sociology, economics, computers, and the fine arts would be a confession of incompetence on the part of any architect. I do not mean to imply that every architect must be an expert in all these matters. There can be just so many Renaissance men, and today's expansion of knowledge, in itself, makes the possibilities of being a universal man almost negligible. But every self-respecting architect must have sufficient general knowledge of all these subjects to enable him to communicate intelligently with his clients and his collaborators.

If the goal of architecture is the design of buildings that produce spaces where people can enjoy thermal, acoustic, and tactile

U.S.A.F. ACADEMY. Sleek articulated forms for which Skidmore, Owings & Merrill are known. Architect: Skidmore, Owings & Merrill.
Photo by Stewarts, Inc.

BRASILIA. Brazil's experiment in the creation of a capital city. Architect: Oscar Niemeyer.
Courtesy of Brazilian Government Trade Center

environments, these should be conceived in man's favor. The end results should influence and affect man's senses so that buildings become, not synthetic atmospheres, but places for people. The complete services of the architect should embrace not only the design of the building proper but all the components of its interior and its environment. This scope includes everything within (decoration, draperies, furniture) and everything without (its impact and effect on the spaces between buildings and on the city in which it stands). Obviously, to fulfill these demands, the architect must nurture and develop his vocabulary throughout his life. The range of his vocabulary is measured by the designs expressed in his buildings.

But before they can be designed and constructed, he must be able to communicate this infinitely varied vocabulary to his generally less technically erudite client. It is not enough to show the client visual presentations. Architecture, like most vocations, has a shorthand jargon of its own whose idiom is immediately understandable to all initiates and to those semi-insiders, engineers and builders, with whom they work. We, as architects, tend to forget that the average layman not only does not understand our jargon but lacks the training and, therefore, the capacity to read our drawings. Not one client in ten, I would wager, knows how to read an architectural plan any more than the average patient understands his doctor's anatomical chart. But most architects overlook this fact in their enthusiasm to show their creations. Consequently, the architect should make it a cardinal rule to master the art of communicating with his client, of translating both graphics and jargon into lay terms.

This is, to me, one of the two meanings of the *language of vision*. The other is the vocabulary of concept, which must be related to Sir Henry Wotton who in 1624 propounded his criteria of firmness, commodity, and delight. He explained that a building must be strong and durable, must be adapted to the needs for which it is built, and must please the eye. To achieve these goals, the architect draws on his experience, his ingenuity, his learning, and his vocabulary to transform the client's fundamental requirements into space relationships. In this way, he hopes to meet the requirements of firmness and commodity through his purely technical vocabulary. His esthetic vocabulary is brought into play in order to satisfy the third criterion —delight. All this, you will recognize at once if you recall your pleasure at the sight of any beautiful structure.

Many architects' reputations arise more from their impact on environment and from the environments they create than from their practical planning abilities. Buildings that work well and are neither outstandingly beautiful nor remarkably ugly are generally taken for granted. It is only when you find it difficult to make your way in a structure or when it strikes the eye by its unusual delight or its utter lack of delight that you take special note of it. If you are interested in architecture, you can soon recognize the work of certain men quite as easily as you can identify the style of Proust or Hemingway without having seen the author's name. Like certain authors, certain architects tend to favor specific vocabularies: the stern, disciplined rigidity of Ludwig Mies van der Rohe; the preoccupation of Frank Lloyd Wright with geometric forms in indigenous materials; the ornamental grillwork of Edward Durell Stone in carved and cast stone; the beautiful use of concrete by Pier Luigi Nervi; the plastic forms of Le Corbusier. Other architects, like the late Eero Saarinen, consciously strove to vary their vocabularies to the maximum and, consequently, few of their designs can be immediately identified.

"FALLING WATER," KAUFMANN RESIDENCE. Wright's genius illustrated in the use of geometric forms. Architect: Frank Lloyd Wright.
Photo by Hedrich-Blessing

In either case, the architect's vocabulary is often restrained and sometimes repressed by factors outside his control. One of the most common is, of course, economics: he cannot exceed his client's budget. Regulations of governmental bodies are almost as frequently oppressive. The tastes of clients often present severe limitations and compel the architect to fall back on a mere fraction of his vocabulary. The man, the company, or the government that is paying the bills tends to view the program of a structure as an inanimate, dry, basically factual set of rules and requirements governed by habits, regulations, and policies calcified by time. But to an architect that same project is alive and dynamic.

One of the most mixed blessings of the past twenty-five years, to the architect's vocabulary, is the wealth and variety of new techniques and manufactured products that he can now employ. But this technical advance has accelerated the demise of craftsmanship in the United States, and without the craftsman the architect is decidedly limited. Even those contemporary architects, with a rich vocabulary of ornamentation and decoration, are largely prevented from using it by the lack of men who can execute their designs. Stonecutters, master cabinet-makers and woodcarvers, marble-setters, ornamental plasterers, and other artisans of past generations have simply disappeared. This is due, in part, to the high cost of individual production. Partly too, perhaps mostly, this reflects the leveling of tastes and the increasing pressures to lose oneself in the

SIMON FRASER UNIVERSITY. Outstanding example of contemporary architecture in a Canadian university. Architect: Erickson/Massey.
Photo by John Fulker

DULLES INTERNATIONAL AIRPORT, VIRGINIA. Architectural expression embracing beautiful forms and eloquent spaces in one of the many idioms which demonstrates Eero Saarinen's wide vocabulary. Architect: Eero Saarinen.
Photo by Joseph W. Molitor

On opposite page

CAMPUS CENTER, RUTGERS UNIVERSITY. Illustrates the use of precast concrete, sculptural in form, with deep reveals; contemporary, yet reminiscent of classical style. Architect: Frank Grad & Sons.
Photo by Gil Amiaga

MINOR SPORTS PALACE. The ingenious use of concrete for both framing and interior design. Architect: Pier Luigi Nervi.
Courtesy of Architectural Forum

anonymous mass. Perhaps we might refer to this anonymity as the fear of excellence that seems to be characteristic of middle-class cultures. Today's architect is seeking expression through space and form devoid of architectural decoration, attempting by the use of shapes of rooms and spaces to create design forms of interest and uniqueness.

This particular form of vocabulary development, however, is frequently throttled by regulations and policies. For example, in designing public and semi-public buildings, we have often sought to create unusual two-story spaces that would add interest to the structures. But these effects are aborted, in many cases, by governmental or insurance regulations. As part of a campus plan for a university, we designed a student center whose main entrance lobby would have been a two-story space around which second-floor rooms would be grouped with a balcony effect. Students entering the building would have the feeling of hospitable space, and those above could look down into it. The university insisted that the

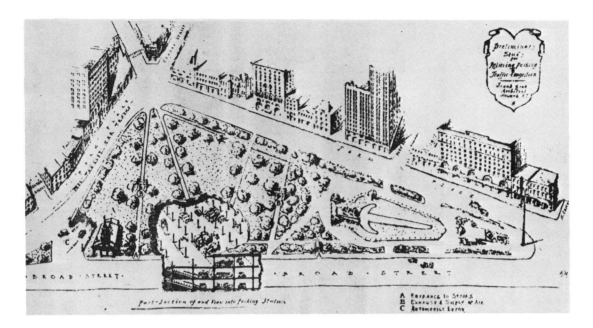

second-floor mezzanine would have to be enclosed in wire glass as a fireproofing measure. An outside balcony, that we had designed to overlook a plaza for academic ceremonies, was ruled out because of the possibility that a student might fall from the balcony. It is curious that in Europe the people do not burn to death or plunge to disaster in the great open spaces that are so often part of the finest buildings.

Public apathy and the influence of the press are often deterrents to people of vision.

In 1927, my father was struck by the rapidly increasing traffic, and, as a consequence, he interested a private client in an underground parking project to accommodate one thousand cars beneath a public park in Newark, New Jersey. The project was priced at $1,500,000 and was presented to the City Fathers for their review and approval. Their subsequent rejection was based in part on an editorial which appeared in the *Newark Evening News:*

MILITARY PARK GARAGE

Tuesday, August 20, 1929.

Much more will have to be revealed about the scheme of Newark and New York backers to construct a three-story sub-surface garage beneath Military Park before intelligent opinion can be passed upon the merits of the plan.

Some such idea has been frequently suggested, it being realized that the construction of a large garage beneath the park would provide parking space for hundreds of cars in the center of the city, thereby

MILITARY PARK UNDERGROUND GARAGE. Preliminary sketch prepared in 1926, shows a three-tiered, underground garage beneath one of Newark's major parks. Architect: Frank Grad & Sons.

MILITARY PARK UNDERGROUND GARAGE. The park surface of the underground garage showing the ramps, kiosks and resurfaced park area. Architect: Frank Grad & Sons.
Photo by Lionel Freedman

affording a convenience to motorists and relieving the streets of congestion.

The construction of such a garage, amounting to a vast tunneling operation in which thousands of cubic feet of earth would have to be removed, would present many difficulties, and certainly involve the expenditure of large sums of money. It is difficult to see how such a scheme could be made financially attractive unless the promoters expect to secure unusual leasing terms from the city. Even if rent was made very nominal by the city, the construction costs of such a structure would be very high. No arrangement would be considered for a minute that did not provide for the maintenance of Military Park in its present condition. This fine old park, the history of which is so entwined with the history of Newark from its earliest day, must not be destroyed or marred, and it is difficult to imagine how a garage could be built beneath it and provided with entrances and exits, ventilating machinery, etc. without damaging the appearance of the park.

Thirty-five years later, the Parking Authority of the City of Newark requested that our office prepare a feasibility study for a one-thousand-car garage under Military Park.

The garage was built at a cost of $5,500,000 and is operating three years ahead of its scheduled income. The grass and the trees are flourishing above it.

Architecture has also suffered as much as it has gained from the American preoccupation with doing everything as economically as possible. Up to the last decade or so, our public works have suffered from mediocrity because of the inherited emphasis on frugality retained from our Puritan forebears. Senators and congressmen alike were responsible for enforcing policies of economy in federal architecture which literally took the delight out of most public buildings.

A client's instructions to milk a design for every last square foot of usable floor space too often deprives the result of any esthetic characteristic. A year or two ago I appeared with another architect on a television program devoted to our profession. My colleague, whose style is more decorative than ours, described how he strives for these ornamental effects. The moderator then asked what I really thought of my own designs that had been shown. Honesty compelled the reply that our buildings were sophisticated boxes that accorded functionally with the wishes of our clients and within these restrictions we strove for an expression of beauty. "Well," the moderator lamented, truthfully, "I guess there is no question that these buildings can hardly be considered art."

Some architects, in the absence of any possibility of decoration, have been clever enough to substitute a rebirth of older styles. Louis Kahn's design for the Salk Institute is reminiscent of an Italian hill town. One group of young men is re-introducing Mayan temple concepts and producing inverted ziggurats. Both are evidence of the search for a form to supplant ornamentation as an identifying mark. There is already a departure from the slick, non-projecting, geometrically-articulated glass wall, that is standard in all big cities. The present trend is toward a virile employment of precast concrete with a minimum of glass, but with deep reveals in which interest is created by deliberately contrived bright highlights and deep shadows.

Encouragingly, interest in architectural improvement is now displayed on a nation-wide basis and on every level of government from the national down to local planning boards. Many states have created councils on the arts; others are following their example. Among their proposals is the endorsement that the budget for every public building include an allocation of 2 to 3 percent of the total cost for sculpture, painting, and other art work that can be incorporated into the total design, thereby fostering collaboration among all the visual arts. Even more important is the change in philosophy among private clients. This newly awakened receptivity to esthetic achievement is coupled with a growing sociological approach to the concept of building.

Frightened by some of the aspects of their phenomenal postwar

NEW JERSEY BELL TELEPHONE COMPANY, HANOVER. Another example of precast concrete where there are few window openings. Architect: Frank Grad & Sons. *Photo by Photog*

growth, many universities and colleges have also stopped to recon-
sider and to plan architecturally with the language of vision. In-
fluenced by the chronic shortage of money, that has always beset
education in this country, many schools have thrown up residence
halls that are mere high-rise barracks with all the impersonality and
frigidity of the average commercial hotel. Such living conditions
have unquestionably contributed in great measure to the unrest on
so many American campuses. It is no coincidence that campus
disturbances have been most frequent and most serious at just those
educational factories where mass production and mass housing are
worst, where everything is done to make the student feel that he has
neither importance nor individuality.

Rutgers is one of the universities that take this problem seri-
ously enough to endeavor to solve it. We were retained, with another firm, to develop for Rutgers a concept of the unit college on a
new campus; a concept that intended to combine the material advantages of the large university with the less tangible assets of the
old-fashioned small college. For a campus of three unit colleges that
would accommodate nine thousand resident students and one thousand day students, we evolved a design that provided an academic
union building for each group of fifteen hundred students. It would

contain the classrooms, faculty offices, student union facilities, and dining accommodations. The residence halls we designed would house no more than fifty students with no more than ten or eleven to a floor. Thus, every student would derive from his environment the sense of belonging to a small college group with which he could identify without sacrificing any of the facilities of the large university. To me, this is the kind of addition to his vocabulary that any architect seeks and welcomes. It is the challenge of creating a new environment.

Opportunities for these challenges are becoming more and more frequent. An outstanding example occurred in 1951 when the Air Force was deeply concerned by the fact that, of the thousands of men it trained at a cost of about $35,000 each, only a handful chose to renew their enlistments. We had been retained to design new Air Force dormitories, mess halls, and headquarters buildings on a standardized basis that would be used throughout the world. It was apparent that the Air Force would do well to take a hard look at all the implications of its existing facilities for enlisted men. These were commonly two- or three-story buildings that contained large dormitories in which forty to sixty men lived, sharing common sanitary

LIVINGSTON COLLEGE, RUTGERS UNIVERSITY. Model showing the dormitories for 1,500 students and the academic center. Architect: Frank Grad & Sons; Anderson, Beckwith & Haible.
Photo by Louis Checkman

facilities; but not all these airmen had the same working hours. Some would be ready for bed at three in the afternoon, others did not start their day until the evening, while the rest began work at seven or eight in the morning. Hence, no one could sleep uninterrupted, and, of course, there was no privacy at all. Congress ignored all pleas for money to remedy the situation. One general, in command at Bolling Field, had to go into business in order to provide suitable facilities for his men. He installed slot machines in mess and recreation areas on an agreement to retain half their "take." When he had amassed $200,000, he divided one barracks into two-man rooms and air-conditioned the whole structure. As a result, he was running a very happy base—despite the opposition of old-line officers to leaving two grown enlisted men, alone and unsupervised, in the same room. The general's example became a prototype; today, Air Force bases around the world afford comfort and privacy to men who need them.

Our experience with the Navy two years later demonstrated the need for versatility of architectural vocabulary. The Bureau of Yards and Docks wanted bachelor officers' quarters at the remote Naval Air Station in Argentia, Newfoundland, to house a thousand men. The standard pattern for officers—unlike enlisted men, it was officially deemed safe to assign them in pairs to rooms—called for three-story walk-up buildings, connected and served by common dining and recreation facilities. In part, this pattern was dictated by economy. Examination showed that the standard line of three-story walk-ups would involve highly expensive foundation work because of the rock characteristics of the site of the building and would be strung out over 1,100 feet in length. Imagine the inconvenience for those officers who lived at the extremities. Here we knew that the logical solution was a high-rise hotel-type structure; since we also knew government red tape, we prepared sketches of our own concept and a scheme embracing the Navy's standards. We then established costs for each and showed the Navy that the high-rise scheme would cost a half-million dollars less than the walk-ups. Here the architect's economic and engineering vocabulary conquered even bureaucratic precedent and resulted in what is now known to Navy personnel as the "Argentia Hilton."

Military design, into which we plunged during World War II, has been a singularly generous contributor to the architectural vocabulary. We were in daily contact with research scientists, innovators of all kinds, mathematicians, and men who were breaking through frontiers. There simply were no precedents, either architec-

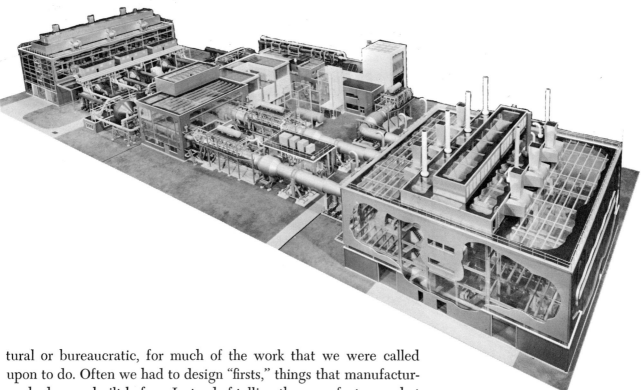

tural or bureaucratic, for much of the work that we were called upon to do. Often we had to design "firsts," things that manufacturers had never built before. Instead of telling the manufacturer what we wanted, how he should build, and what materials he should use, we could tell him only the function that his product must perform. It was up to him to determine the rest. The results have immeasurably enriched the profession's vocabulary.

A delicate problem confronts the architect when it is the client's vocabulary that is archaic. In our first assignments for the New Jersey Bell Telephone Company we found that its book of standards was eminently valid for the time in which it had been compiled, but bore little relevance to the drastically changed conditions of the present. Most telephone buildings, except those housing personnel, contain fantastically expensive equipment whose protection is paramount in building design. We found, however, that the walls of telephone-company buildings were needlessly and expensively thick. The company agreed to review our proposed studies of wall construction with a view to equal protection at lower first cost and cheaper maintenance. As a result we were able to improve the design of these structures. But precedent—or the lack of precedent, to be more accurate—aborted a subsequent effort.

The same company commissioned us to design a large accounting center in a park-like setting. Its standard was a building of two stories and basement, rectangular and compact. We received authorization to re-evaluate the design concept and evolved a plan based on both the generous site and the work flow of accounting procedures. This called for an exclusively horizontal design which eliminated all vertical traffic and concentrated the service utilities,

U.S. NAVY, AIR TURBINE TEST STATION, WEST TRENTON, NEW JERSEY. Model served to coordinate the architectural and extremely complicated engineering concept, and was used for orientation and demonstration by Naval personnel who would operate the actual test facilities. Architect: Frank Grad & Sons; Jaros, Baum & Bolles; Burns & Roe, Inc., a Joint Venture.
Photo by Morris Rosenfeld

Examples of design problems requiring unusual engineering research.

U.S.A.F., Airmen's Dormitory Complex, Ernest Harmon Air Force Base, Newfoundland. Three high-rise dormitory buildings, designed on the basis of two men to each room, which contain mess and recreation facilities. Architect: Frank Grad & Sons.

U.S.A.F., Snark Missile Facility, Presque Isle, Maine. Architect: Frank Grad & Sons; Urbahn, Brayton & Burrows; Seelye, Stevenson, Value & Knecht.

U.S.A.F., Design of Hardened, Tactical Missile-Launching Facilities. Architect: Frank Grad & Sons; Urbahn, Brayton & Burrows; Seelye, Stevenson, Value & Knecht.

NEW JERSEY BELL TELEPHONE COMPANY, EWING TOWNSHIP. This two-story and basement structure was the acceptable solution. Architect: Frank Grad & Sons.

but the model that we built from our schematic drawings was rejected because such a thing had never before been done by the company. They had always clung to the two-stories-and-basement model. In the years since this disappointment, however, the American Telephone & Telegraph Company, Western Electric, and the New Jersey Bell System have liberalized their instructions to architects on the sound principle that the architect can contribute substantially to the advancement of design. Now AT&T holds periodic competitions and gives awards to its subsidiary companies and their architects for "Excellence in Architecture at Low Cost, with due regard for Simplicity and Appropriateness to Site and Environment."

The language of vision is far from static. Every day new words are coined and added to its vocabulary. Take the case of a new dimension in education, the community college, an outgrowth of our junior college. Educators predict that ten years from now six million students will be enrolled in new community colleges on urban and suburban campuses. Records show that two-year colleges are being activated at the rate of one each week.

The design of these educational facilities is one of the newer challenges to architects. Not only are educators faced with the development of educational specifications which program the disciplines to be taught in community colleges, but architects must become knowledgeable in planning these facilities so as to skillfully design complexes within which these new techniques of education can be accommodated.

An example of our own higher educational involvement is the design of the Bergen County Community College in Paramus, New Jersey. In pursuing the philosophy that the community college is the student's "home away from home," where he or she can spend an entire day within an academic environment, the concept of a "mega-structure" has been developed.

This college, on a beautiful 170-acre golf course, is a series of interconnected departments, flexible in design in order to accommodate future interchanges. A student can reach all of the facilities within the complex and not be forced to leave the building.

Today we know that, as architects, we must take the time to attend seminars and meetings embracing the academic and other extensive worlds. The sophisticated sciences of our society demand familiarization with new and future techniques if we are to be qualified to compete with our colleagues for commissions in the more exotic fields.

A new and wondrous area lies in the domain of the computer, a positive factor in all of our lives. Large corporations such as IBM and AT&T have commissioned us to design computer centers for their use. Without some understanding of how they work, it is impossible for an architect to design enclosed space for them. Again, the necessity appears for members of our staff to involve themselves in continuing education to learn the nature, functions, and requirements of man's most recent creations.

There is, of course, frequent conflict between the architect's desire to force his concepts on his client, and the client's determination to shape the buildings for which he is paying. Men and companies with experience in construction expansion, are likely to arrive much more quickly at a meeting of minds with the architect. But sometimes the client who has never commissioned a building, who must put himself wholly in his architect's hands, finds himself the owner of a most unsatisfactory experiment. It is as unwise for the architect to force his theories on the client as it is for the client to dictate rigidly to the architect. Communication between them, from the start of their relationship, is essential, but is not always easily achieved—least of all when a multiplicity of approving bodies must be contended with.

In 1961, before former President Kennedy had appointed his new Fine Arts Commission, we were commissioned, in a joint venture with Curtis & Davis of New Orleans and Fordyce & Hamby of New York, to design a new federal office building in Washington,

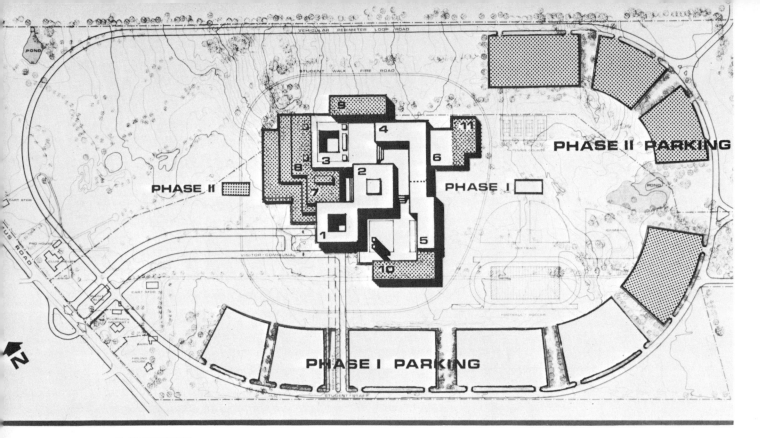

LEGEND

PHASE I	PHASE II
1 ADMINISTRATION	7 FINE ARTS
2 LIBRARY	8 STUDENT UNION
3 STUDENT UNION	9 SCIENCE
4 SCIENCE	10 HUMANITIES
5 HUMANITIES	11 PHYS. ED.
6 PHYS. ED.	

Techcrete, Hypothetical Demonstration Model for the Department of Defense Proposal. Experiment in design and construction of housing using the "systems" approach. Architect: Carl Koch & Associates, Inc.
Photo by George Zimberg

On opposite page:
Top

Bergen Community College. A preliminary site plan indicating Phases I and II. Architect: Frank Grad & Sons.

Bottom

Bergen Community College. Preliminary model of the mega-building. Architect: Frank Grad & Sons.
Photo by Louis Checkman

D.C. The client was the General Services Administration, which has jurisdiction over most federal buildings. GSA furnished us with a brief criteria as to site, the square footage of the building, and the budget. We were not told which governmental agency would be the user of the building. We were told that it was to be of the "garden variety" type, and that the design must remain in consonance with the extensive redevelopment program under way in the capital. The site was bisected by a street which, at that time, the planners contemplated making into a mall. An adjacent project was under the sponsorship of a prominent real-estate developer designated by the Redevelopment Land Agency to transform a portion of southwest Washington into an architectural dream. Indeed, great progress in this direction had already been made with the replacement of slums by attractive office and residential areas.

Our task was not eased by the fact that twenty-seven different government entities had voices in the matter, not merely the GSA and the agency that would use the building—the Department of Defense, as it later turned out—but all the municipal departments concerned with construction, as well as a number of federal bodies. After an exhaustive study of all the factors bearing on the problem, those of environment as well as those of use, we concluded that, despite the division of the site into halves by the proposed Tenth Street Mall, the solution was not the conventional one of buildings on both sides of the mall. Instead, we planned a main tower building of six stories that would be supported on columns so that its first floor would be thirty-three feet above the mall—a light, airy structure floating in repose, rather than a ponderous mass. It was to be flanked by parallel buildings on each side of the mall; all to be linked by a simple neck or bridge.

This deployment of the architectural vocabulary was favorably received by the GSA and the National Capitol Planning Commission; the Fine Arts Commission, composed of traditional architects, objected that our design was not in harmony with Washington architecture. But the real resistance came from the source that had least to do with the building and absolutely no jurisdiction over it, the real-estate developer. He denounced our vast conspiracy to erect a Chinese wall sealing off his project. While his fulminations were still re-echoing—with considerable assistance from his public relations henchmen—the President appointed an entirely new Fine Arts Commission. The new group, composed of experts in the con-

JAMES FORRESTAL BUILDING, WASHINGTON, D.C. Preliminary site plan of the original scheme showing the six-story "tower" building, spanning the 10th Street Mall, and two symmetrical buildings flanking the Mall. Associated Architects: Curtis & Davis; Fordyce and Hamby Associates; Frank Grad & Sons.
Photo by Louis Checkman

JAMES FORRESTAL BUILDING, WASHINGTON, D.C. View from Independence Avenue of an early study model showing the design developed with the intent of achieving a light, buoyant building resting on "umbrella" columns. Associated Architects: Curtis & Davis; Fordyce and Hamby Associates; Frank Grad & Sons.
Photo by Ezra Stoller

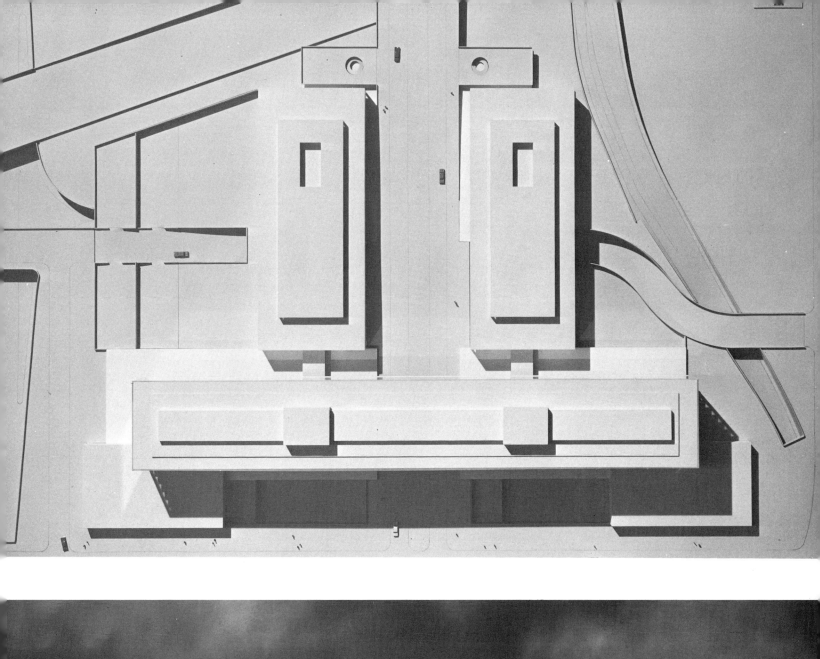

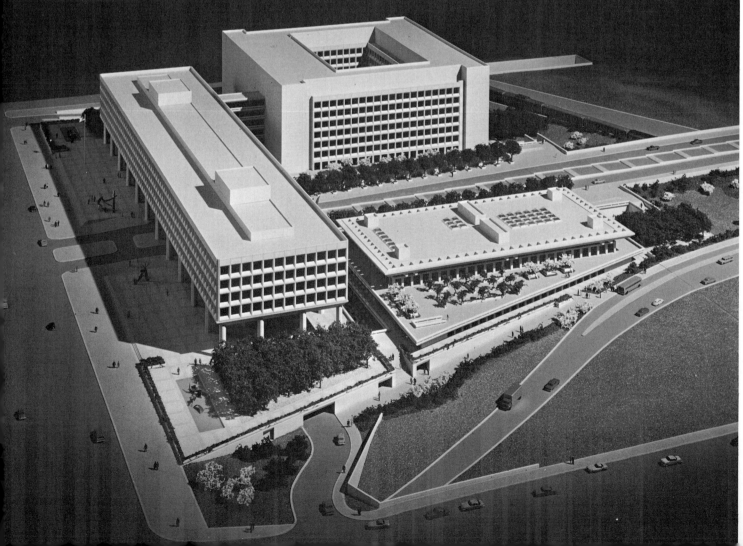

temporary idiom, thought highly of our scheme. Then a new man joined the commission.

In ten minutes, the work of eighteen months was destroyed—despite the outcries of the GSA. The new appointee had his own vocabulary into which our ideas apparently could not be translated. It appeared at first that the whole project must be redesigned, and our contracts were renegotiated accordingly. In the end, by reducing it to four stories, we saved the floating tower. Behind this, on the east side of the mall we designed what we called an inside-out building, the sheer masonry of its exterior divided in a striated pattern to relieve its massiveness; and its windows facing inward on a landscaped court. It was connected to the tower by a link. On the opposite side of the mall we placed a small jewel of a cafeteria so that the inside-out structure at the rear would be a complete foil for the precast concrete tower, and the sparkling small cafeteria would afford a space relation compatible with the total concept. Four years after we began to study the program, construction was begun, in July of 1965.

An exercise in frustration? Only on the surface. Maddening as the long struggle was, I would not have missed it for anything. Not only did it reward us with the gratification that comes from riding out a seemingly impossible situation, but it was one more valuable and enjoyable lesson in vocabulary-building.

Top

JAMES FORRESTAL BUILDING, WASHINGTON, D.C. View of the model in site-plan form showing the final design comprised of three units: a four-story "tower" spanning the 10th Street Mall, a ten-story doughnut building east of the Mall and the cafeteria building on the west side. Associated Architects: Curtis & Davis; Fordyce and Hamby Associates; Frank Grad & Sons.
Photo by Louis Checkman

Bottom

JAMES FORRESTAL BUILDING, WASHINGTON, D.C. View of the model looking east along Independence Avenue showing the three-unit concept of the Forrestal Building. Associated Architects: Curtis & Davis; Fordyce and Hamby Associates; Frank Grad & Sons.
Photo by Ezra Stoller

7. *Infernal Eternities*

One morning in 1951, while discussing staff problems, my father remarked that according to the morning paper, Congress was preparing to vote funds for a number of new Air Force installations in Europe, and, he added, an Air Force officer with whom we had worked was now stationed in Wiesbaden, in charge of European operations.

"Why not call him?" I said.

"You mean right now?" My father was startled. Our operator was equally surprised when he asked her to place the call; such conversations had not yet become commonplace in our office.

The following Tuesday my father and brother were in Wiesbaden; within two weeks they were back in Newark with a contract for the preliminary designs for four air bases in France.

Believe me, this is the exception, not the norm. In 1963 there were only nine thousand architectural offices in the whole country, and more than four thousand had no employees. With an average staff of eight people, few offices can afford to seek out-of-state, let alone international, assignments. In small partnerships or large, the average day is quite different from the morning I have described, and our own office is fairly representative of the profession as a whole.

Once every two weeks we hold a staff meeting, from nine until ten-thirty in the morning. It is attended by all partners, associates, and key personnel, and includes any project manager or job captain who may have a matter on which to report. The staff meeting reviews every project that we have in work. The man in charge of each job details its progress in design or production. If the project requires information from the client or a consultant, or if some aspect of it must be resolved with a governmental agency, the partners assign such tasks to the men who are most qualified and closest to the situation. Calendars are established for meetings with clients, personnel assignments are reviewed, and our internal budget, the bloodstream of our organization, is studied.

Our accounting department collects all the time cards from our personnel for every two-week period and posts the figures against each job. Charges and expenses of a direct technical nature and the non-technical supporting overhead items are then tallied. In this way we have a running score of the cost of each project. This is probably the most difficult of all our tasks: creative and technical people hate to be bothered with such prosaic chores as recording time and expenditures. But business management is as vital to the architect as to the soap manufacturer. If it is not practiced properly and daily, the architect simply trusts to luck that he will close the year with a profit. To strengthen our own management practices, we called on a firm of management consultants to make a ruthless study of our operations, and, while its disclosures of management errors may have embarrassed us, we have benefited from it ever since. Everything in which an architect is engaged, after all, is governed by business principles, and he must apply them to the marketing of the two things he has to sell: time and talent. If they are not used correctly, budgeted properly, and stripped of waste, the architect will find that his most valuable assets are being irrevocably dissipated.

After the staff meeting, unless I have to leave the offices for outside appointments, I devote the next half-hour to going over incoming mail and previously prepared reports, and routing each to the appropriate individual. At the same time, I schedule replies in the order of urgency. Since I try not to accept telephone calls until eleven, I then check with the switchboard and make whatever calls are necessary. Invariably, I find myself wondering whether to bless or curse the telephone, which, with paper-moving, seems to consume virtually all of everyone's working time. The two are inter-related since every inside or outside meeting, by office rule, is recorded in minutes, which are studied at staff conferences and which are invaluable references for the incessant telephoning or for subsequent meetings.

Special problems have a special time, roughly the period be-

tween eleven-thirty and noon, when they are discussed with my
partners and associates. These more intimate meetings may also
deal with new business or some urgent field problem; often they are
devoted to subjects, developed in staff conferences, that require
more consideration by the people at the top. Once special-problem
time has passed, there is another check with the switchboard,
usually followed by the return of important calls, before I can safely
go to lunch, which is rarely unmixed relaxation. It is almost always a
further time for a conference with a client, with partners, with some
civic organization, with our lawyer, or our public relations counsel.
When work is frenetic, lunch is inhaled at my desk, and dessert takes
the form of more telephoning.

It is only in the afternoon that I can spare the time from
administration to get into the design department. I try to spend at

U.S. Air Force Base, Laon Couvron, France. One of the bases under
NATO command located in northeastern France. Architect: Frank
Grad & Sons; Seelye, Stevenson, Value & Knecht.
Photo by Sickles Photo Reporting Service

least two hours a day reviewing, with our chief designer and his
staff, all the projects that are under development. I find this interval
the most rewarding part of the day. In such sessions I can translate
the minutes of a meeting with a client into my own concept on
which the design team will work. This, too, is the time when we
must often perform drastic architectural surgery on a program too
big for its budget. These hours are given over, as it were, to the pure
practice of architecture, as distinguished from administering an
architectural office.

From four to four-thirty I try to expedite the outgoing mail.
And, in the half-hour before the office officially closes, the telephone once more occupies most of my attention, this time without
resentment; these are the calls that so often can take the place of
further meetings. At the end of the day, when most of the staff has

gone home, I am, at last, free to attend to non-technical problems: personnel, field emergencies, contractor troubles, and countless others. But I can rarely let myself out of the office with the feeling that I have really accomplished everything that was on my day's agenda. That is one of the reasons why I welcome, rather than resent, the two hours of daily commuting. On the train I can think absolutely undisturbed. I can attempt to catch up with my professional reading, review office papers and designs, and even sketch. The sketch pad in the architect's pocket is as important as the other man's memorandum book. Ideas, verbal or visual, come at their own time and convenience. More than once I have caught myself tracing a design in the mirror with one hand, while I was shaving with the other.

All the architect's days are by no means spent in the office. There are continual meetings with clients, consultants, and governmental officials. One never stops learning. Every client's business and needs differ. It is by no means unusual for a busy architect to find himself involved, more or less simultaneously, with education, medicine, religion, manufacturing, transportation, publishing, communications, recreation, military affairs, sports, and a host of other fields. This learning acquaintance, which often becomes familiarity and sometimes intimacy, begins with the abstract discussion of the client's program. Its lasting impress, however, comes from the repeated inspections that the architect must make while the construction is in progress. In the field, he is the archetype of the man in the middle; if things are not going as they should, both the owner and the contractor are going to blame him exclusively.

Besides verifying the contractor's work and certifying it so that the contractor may be paid, the architect must also observe progress and anticipate any additions to the project that necessitate further outlays. Not only must he assist in interpreting plans and specifications to the contractor and subcontractors, he must also resolve any disputes that, legitimately or otherwise, arise. As we saw earlier, there are dozens of trades involved in every building. Orderly construction must depend on a sequential procedure of operations. For instance, when the contractor is raising a reinforced concrete or structural frame, he must insert holes or chases in the walls, floors, and foundations for the "spaghetti"—the plumbing and heating lines, the electrical conduits, and the air conditioning ducts. Very often the subcontractors find themselves in sharp conflict on priority of work, and, on the spot, the architect must sometimes move some functions of the building in order to permit the installation of others without impingement. Ideally, these problems are resolved at the regular job meetings in the field, attended by representatives of the owner, the architect, and all the various trades.

The architect must also constantly check the standards of workmanship. Until the recent vogue for exposed masonry in interiors, the practice of plastering inside walls inevitably covered up a good many sins of what may charitably be called substandard workmanship; but when exposed masonry is used, it is of paramount importance that these surfaces be laid up correctly. One of our inspectors was so meticulous that he became the mortal enemy of most of our contractors. He would check every surface with a penknife or a visiting card to make sure it had been properly "buttered"—coated with mortar so as to bed solidly with the unit below it.

This man was a handsome, impressive architect who dressed impeccably—somewhat too impeccably for the taste of many of the masons. But they had their revenge. After he whipped out his knife or card to check the buttering the men would expertly flick the excess mortar off their trowels in such a manner that it hit the ground a few feet behind him, spattering the back of his suit so softly that he did not even feel it. Very often he finished his day with a collar-to-cuff stripe down his back.

Another of our field representatives was almost universally called the fussiest architect of his time. One of his duties was to prepare a punch list—an inventory of items that must be completed before the architect can issue his final certificate for a project. The contractor always hopes that this will consist of nothing more than the usual odds and ends that he already knows must be cleared up. But our man was so thorough that he insisted on checking even the paint on the tops and bottoms of doors. Obviously, he could not command that a ladder be brought to each door so that he could see the top, nor, once the door was hung, could he see the underside even if he lay on the floor. So he carried a dental mirror! Any architect whose contractor finds him using instruments of this kind may be sure that his projects will be stolen bare in some other aspect.

In a sense, a day in the field can be a day of acrobatics, for the architect must walk a tight-rope. He cannot afford to antagonize contractors nor can he afford to overlook their delinquencies. All his diplomacy—like all the tact and finesse of the orchestra conductor of my earlier comparison—must be employed not only to arbitrate

Smith House, Darien, Connecticut.
Example of the vitality and dynamism of
the new young breed of American architect. Architect: Richard Meier.
Photo by Ezra Stoller

among conflicting subcontractors, but to expedite a job that is lag-
ging. A dissatisfied owner turns naturally to the architect to answer
for inadequate progress. At the job meetings the architect can ascer-
tain the reasons for the delay—for example, some trades are under-
manned, or certain materials have not arrived on schedule—then,
with the contractor and subcontractors, he can plan corrective
measures.

However harassing a day in the field may be, equally nerve-
racking is the time spent with the committee or individual who is
passing on findings prepared by the architect as a result of his field
inspection. The simplest example, and one of the most frequent, is
that of the architect commissioned to design a residence for a couple
who have decided on a fixed maximum expenditure. The husband is
firm on this score; but, as the drawings develop, the wife begins to
do what architects call "the creep"; she wants to enlarge the living
room, to add a bathroom, to turn the kitchen into a display of major
appliances. Little by little, with only the merest and vaguest hint to
her husband, she has folded additional thousands of dollars into
what started out as a reasonable project.

A complex institutional or corporate program that is afflicted
with "the creep" can make the problem far more serious. A large
university, for which we have done work over the years, has a
typical chain of command: the president, the board of governors,
the finance and budget committee, the building and grounds com-

mittee, the department of new facilities, the consulting architect of the university, and various program committees. The opportunities thus presented to "the creep" are almost limitless. Two instances in particular come to mind.

One involved food service facilities that, as the responsible official demonstrated, would increase the required square footage by one-third. The other arose out of the sound conviction of the chemistry professors that their proposed new building was ten thousand square feet too small. Naturally, both instances resulted in substantial budget increases that had to be approved by the committee with ultimate responsibility. Months of re-evaluation and arduous study preceded the meeting at which we submitted the revised budget. Before a group of knowledgeable and hard-headed men, who were expert in balancing economics with the ultimate goals of the university, we set out to prove concisely why we had to exceed their budget by a million dollars in order to design what the university needed.

The committee's affirmative reaction, I am convinced, had a certain intuitive as well as a highly rational basis. As animals can smell human fear, committees seem to scent architectural unpreparedness. When that meeting began, had we not been in a position to logically answer every objection, the whole project would have bogged down indefinitely in a fruitless effort to determine whose fault it was that we had to exceed the budget.

But not every client committee is knowledgeable or understanding or, in many cases, especially eager to learn. There are days in every architect's life that are infernal eternities when he is almost ready to swear that, from morning to night, he has been battling an invincible determination to understand nothing. This intransigence extends into areas other than program and budget as we learned most painfully when we were retained to design New Jersey's State Cultural Center. Soon afterward, some officials involved decided that all concerned needed the assistance of a number of advisory committees. Out of this decision came a request that our firm accept, as a consultant, an internationally known architect with prior experience in such projects. Very reluctantly we acceded. We had long since learned that unless architects make such mutual arrangements before a commission is sought or accepted, the architect-consultant will automatically feel that without his help everything would collapse.

Many of the men we canvassed—all of them acceptable to the

state—were too busy to accept. The architect, who was finally approved by the state as well as by us, had agreed that he would do no more than advise us, and that the project concept would be our function. In spite of our understanding, once we were at work, he insisted that he was to be the star of the performance. The situation was grave, and it was not amenable to negotiation. There was no choice but to place the problem before the State Commissioner of Education. He suggested that our only hope lay in a presentation to the advisory board requesting that it rescind the requirement for a consultant. I did not at once embrace this plan; it seemed to require a blatant self-advertisement that was not only embarrassing to me, but might well antagonize those to whom it was addressed. But the commissioner assured me that the latter result, at least, was most unlikely.

Consequently, I appeared before a most impressive board and attempted to explain concisely and rationally why we could not accept the present arrangement: a forcible revision of our commission by an outsider who wanted to turn us into mere drones to his concepts when by our own professional record, we were fully qualified to be sole architect for the project. The commissioner then polled each member of the board, and for two hours I listened to their crossfire of arguments. Finally, the commissioner called on Dr. William Dix, Chief Librarian of Princeton University, whom I had never met. Dr. Dix began by declaring that in all his years as a consultant on library projects, he had learned less about the workings of an architect's office than he had just absorbed in the past two hours. Then he addressed me: "Mr. Grad, may I give you one piece of advice? Design this facility as you see it and do not listen to anyone in this room who has only a cursory knowledge of architecture. Otherwise you will wind up with the kind of mediocrity that covers all our college campuses." He concluded by turning back to the full board and proposing, in essence, that, since we had been retained to design the Cultural Center, we proceed to do so as first-class, not second-class, citizens.

That was all that Dr. Dix had to say. The commissioner called for a vote, and it was unanimous: we were to go on with our business without any consultant.

Mutual respect and loyalty should be prime requisites in the day-to-day practice of architecture. During the Second World War we were commissioned to design, among other facilities, a dispensary for a naval air station. The officer in charge was a recently commissioned lieutenant who had taught engineering in a university and had no construction experience. Having finished our design, we submitted our work for approval and went on to the next project. For four days the former professor did not appear. At the end of that time, he marched into my office, threw the roll of drawings on my desk and announced: "I've been revising these at home. Make the corrections and I'll send them to the naval district for approval." Thereupon he whipped around and strode out.

Working my way through his multicolored crayon markings, which made the drawings look like Guatemalan postage stamps, I found that he had nowhere indicated our designs or concepts were wrong. He simply wanted them done differently. His corrections were all of the same order: where we specified half-inch reinforcing rods in a concrete foundation, he changed them to five-eighths-inch, spaced further apart. Mastering my initial anger, I went and informed him that we did not intend to make substitutions for things that were correct and, as the duly licensed and commissioned architects, we were responsible. If he chose to dispute the matter, I would take it to his superiors. He backed down, but I had acquired an enemy. On the other hand, his attitude toward us was no different from his behavior toward everyone else. Within a few days, all thirty architectural firms working for this naval district were called to a meeting with all officers involved in construction. The admiral, who had initiated the meeting, apologized for interrupting our work, and explained that he wanted us to hear his orders to his officers: their function as officers in charge of construction for the Bureau of Yards and Docks was 95 percent administrative and 5 percent technical. The meeting was then adjourned.

On the other hand, an officer in a similar position at a naval supply depot began our first conversation this way: "Grad, I have just been commissioned a lieutenant commander. This is my first station after indoctrination. I'm a highway engineer and I think I can hold my own with anyone in that field. But I've never before been connected with building design or construction. As far as I'm concerned, you and your firm are the experts in designing these new facilities. Since the Navy retained you to do so, I'll take all the counsel and advice you want to offer."

Those are the moments that an architect treasures.

8. A Typical Project—
The New Jersey Cultural Center

In Chapter 3, I outlined the step-by-step operation of an architect's *modus operandi*. In this chapter, the development of the New Jersey Cultural Center will be explained in a minor way verbally and in a major fashion graphically. It is, of course, impossible to describe all of the work that takes place on any project, but I believe the high spots will be covered here so that the important functions of the architect's work come alive.

Before getting into any of the details, it is interesting to take note of the fact that this project was started in February, 1961, completed and formally dedicated in September, 1965—an elapsed time of four and one-half years. The timetable of the major intervals between the two dates is instructive.

A brief history of the nature of the project is in order as a preamble, and this story is best unfolded by a description of the site on which the project was to be located and an outline of the program for the Center describing its goals.

The site lies directly west of the existing State House Annex and is part of the major complex of state buildings in Trenton. It posed an interesting challenge because it is bounded on the north by State Street, the main thoroughfare of the city of Trenton, and on the south by the John Fitch Way express highway, with a difference in elevation from State Street to John Fitch Way of 15 feet. Because of its location between these two major streets, the facility would have neither a front nor a back door, for it would be equally accessible to the public from both streets. The site had a number of magnificent old trees which had to be retained and protected during construction and, naturally, would afford great enhancement to the design.

The program, which was prepared in depth by officials of both the museum and the library, envisioned a highly flexible multi-purpose institution primarily symbolic of the state's progressive attitude toward public education, and was set up to embrace a museum in which a small auditorium was to be contained, a library and a planetarium. These facilities were to be supported by parking areas and landscaping. The goals described in the program were specified by seven directives:

1. To tell the story of the state's natural and human resources in relation to their social and economic significance.

2. To provide adequately for the growing throngs of school children who would visit the museum every year.

3. To make available for study and research not only the material to be put on exhibit but also the many and vast geological, paleontological, archeological, and zoological collections that had been inaccessible for years.

4. To provide an auditorium for the public enjoyment of programs giving added depth to the museum's exhibits and for the presentation of the performing arts.

5. To increase public participation in museum services and facilities by making them available for such activities as evening lectures, workshops for adults, and weekend programs and demonstrations.

6. To offer a planetarium of sufficient scope to be a vital source of scientific information.

7. To provide a state library that would be capable of: offering a general reference and law library; providing legislative reference and research services; promoting local library services throughout the state; preserving New Jersey's basic historical documents, and supervising and retaining of the state's public records and those of its political subdivisions.

From February to October, 1961, we were engaged in a study of the program and were relating the specified requirements to the funds which had been appropriated. During this period of evaluation, it became apparent that there were insufficient funds to provide for the projected auditorium and planetarium. It was not until March, 1962 that this problem was resolved by the state and additional funds appropriated so that the total program could be included in the design concept. In October, 1962, the final working

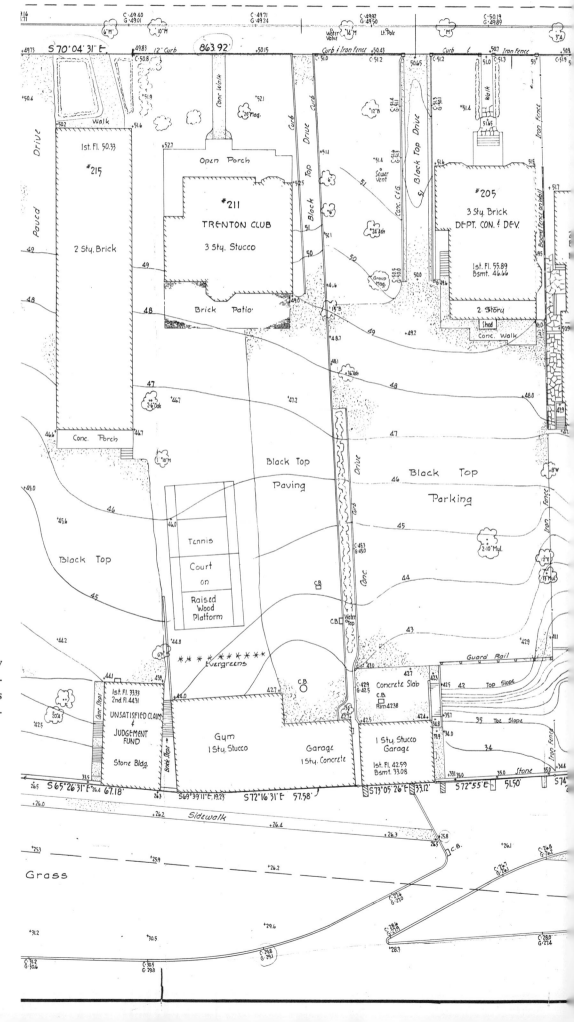

EXHIBIT I. The topographical survey of the site showing its location, physical contours, trees, existing buildings to be removed, and sub-surface utilities.

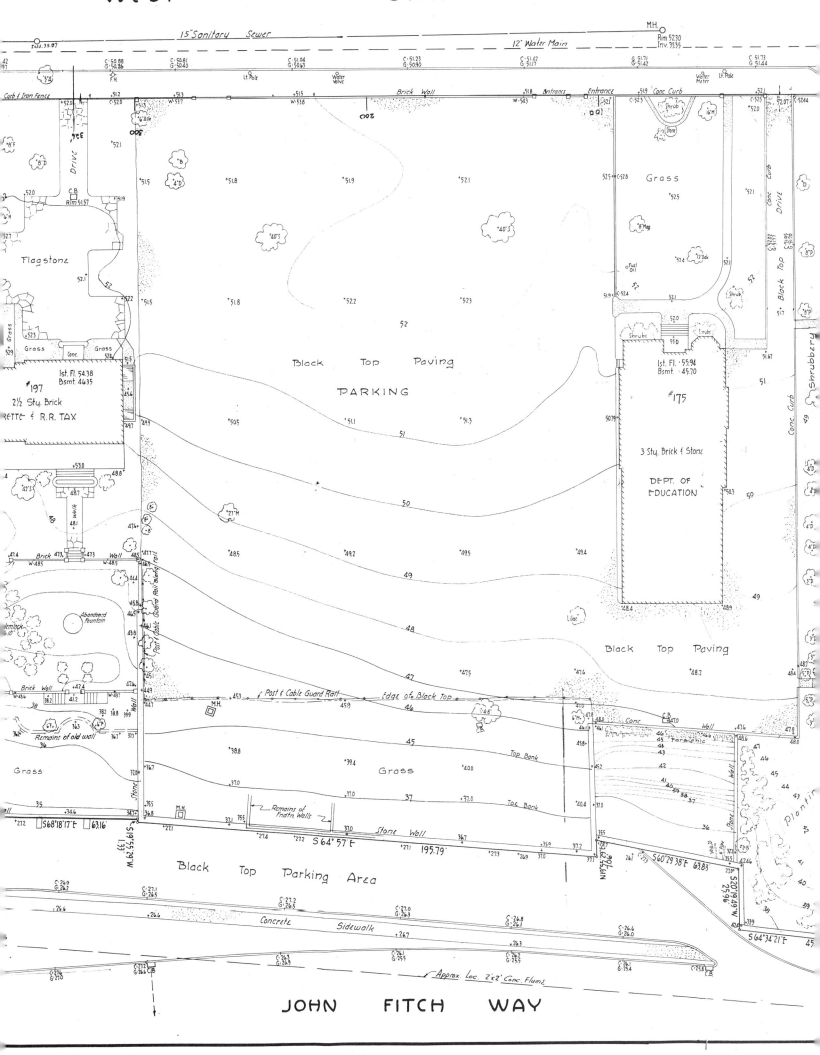

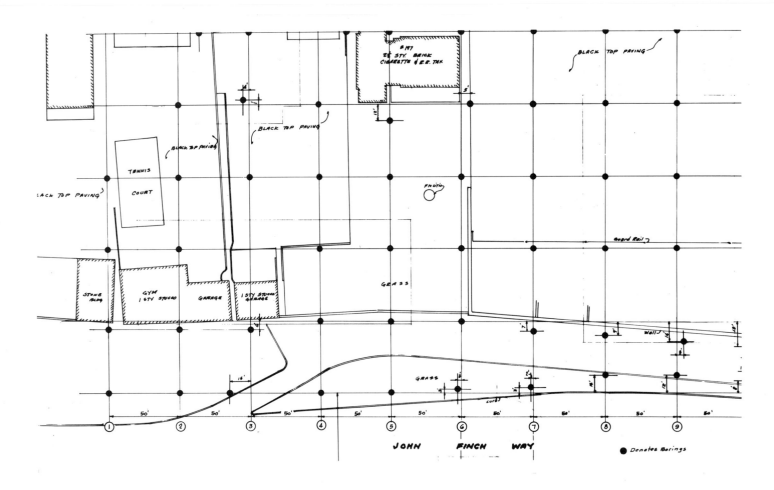

JOHN FINCH WAY

● Denotes Borings

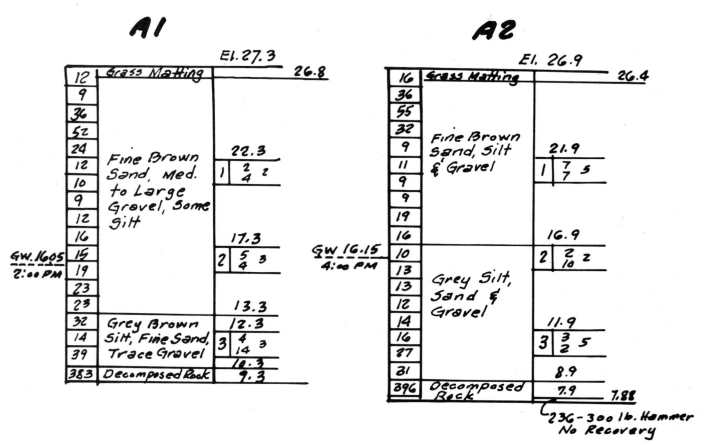

A1

El. 27.3

26.8

12	Grass Matting
9	
36	
52	
24	Fine Brown	22.3
12	Sand, Med.	1	2	2
			4	
10	to Large	
9	Gravel, Some	
12	Silt	
16		17.3
15		2	5	3
19			4	
23		
23		13.3
32	Grey Brown	12.3
14	Silt, Fine Sand,	3	4	3
39	Trace Gravel		14	
		10.3
383	Decomposed Rock	9.3

GW. 1605
2:00 PM

A2

El. 26.9

26.4

16	Grass Matting
36	
55	
32	
9	Fine Brown	21.9
11	Sand, Silt	1	7	5
	& Gravel		7	
9		
9		
19		
16		16.9
10		2	2	2
13			10	
13	Grey Silt,	
12	Sand &	
14	Gravel	11.9
16		3	3	5
87			2	
31		8.9
396	Decomposed Rock	7.9	7.88

GW 16.15
4:00 PM

236 - 300 lb. Hammer
No Recovery

EXHIBIT II. A partial boring log indicating the sub-surface soils revealed by a series of bore holes which covered the site on a 50′ grid.

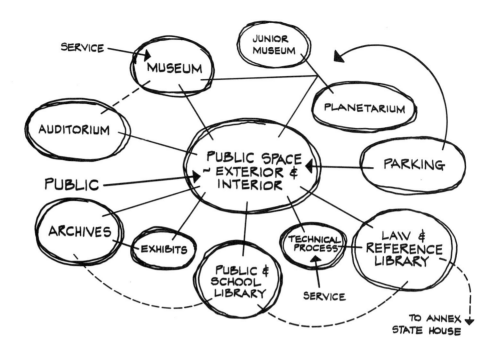

Exhibit III. A bubble diagram showing the space relationships of the major facilities in the complex of buildings.

Exhibit IV. A bubble diagram showing the space relationships of the junior museum and the planetarium.

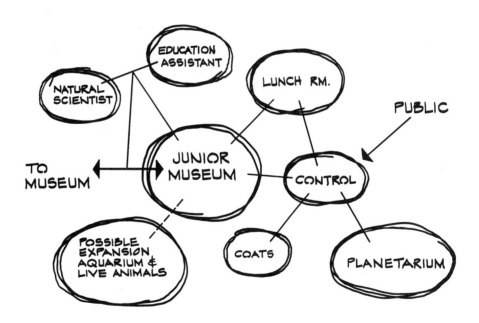

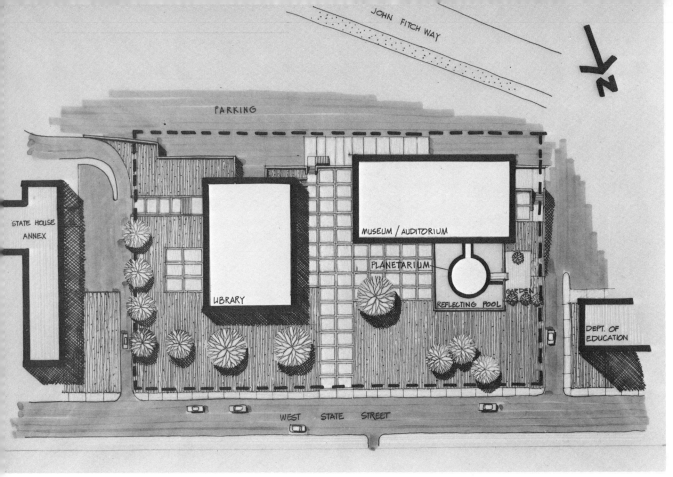

V

VI

Exhibit V. A preliminary site plan which was developed during the early stages of the program evaluation when the auditorium was included within the museum.

Exhibit VI. A perspective study in mass, reflecting the site plan in Exhibit V.

Exhibit VII. A preliminary site plan showing the development with the auditorium as a separate facility.

Exhibit VIII. A perspective rendering in mass, showing the disposition of the major elements indicated in VII.

Exhibit IX. A preliminary cross-section showing the relationships of the auditorium, museum, and planetarium with respect to State Street and John Fitch Way.

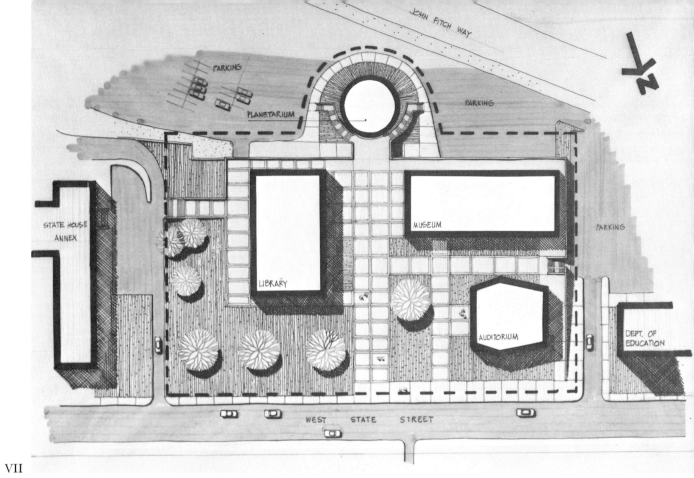

PARKING

JOHN FITCH WAY

PLANETARIUM

PARKING

STATE HOUSE ANNEX

MUSEUM

PARKING

LIBRARY

AUDITORIUM

DEPT. OF EDUCATION

WEST STATE STREET

VII

VIII

IX

OFFICES

EXHIBITS

PLANETARIUM

MUSEUM

AUDITORIUM

WEST STATE STREET

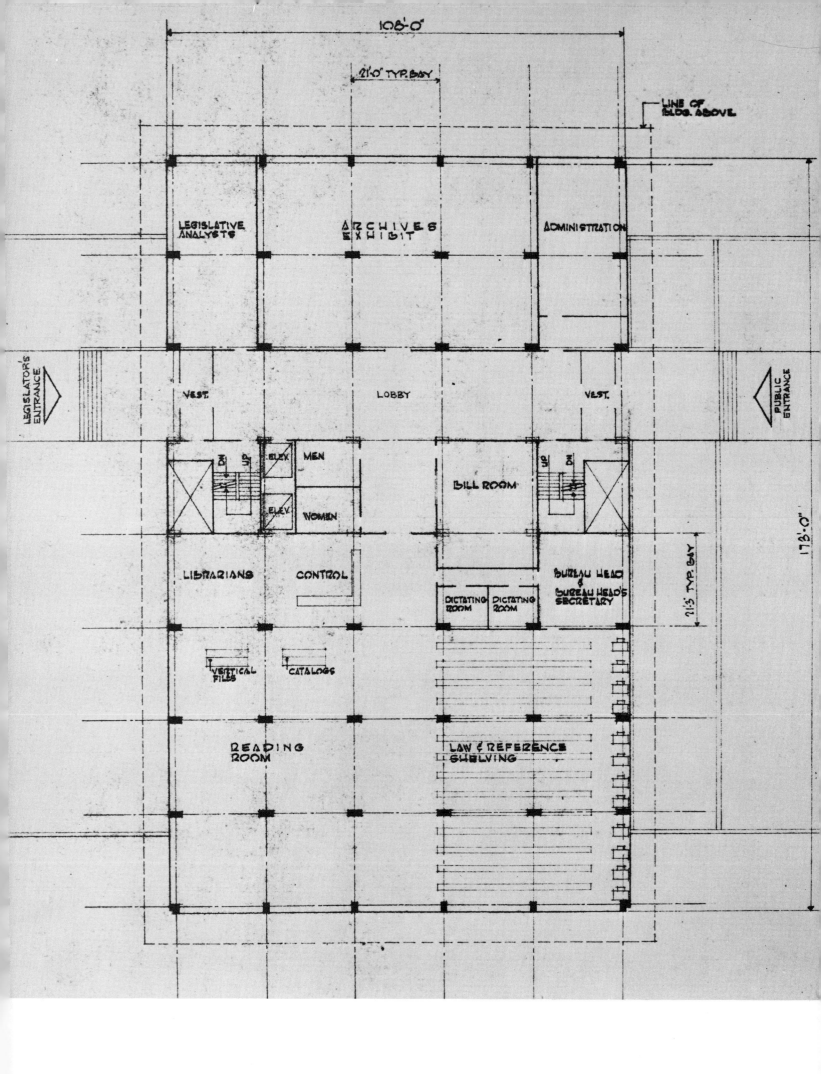

EXHIBIT X. A sketch typical of a preliminary drawing of the first floor plan of the library on which all of the facilities on this floor plan are sufficiently dimensioned in accordance with the structural system and the bay spacing which had been studied and adopted.

EXHIBIT XI. A photo of the final model which accompanied the preliminary drawings which formed a part of the package along with the final budget estimate when the architects received approval to proceed with the final working drawings.

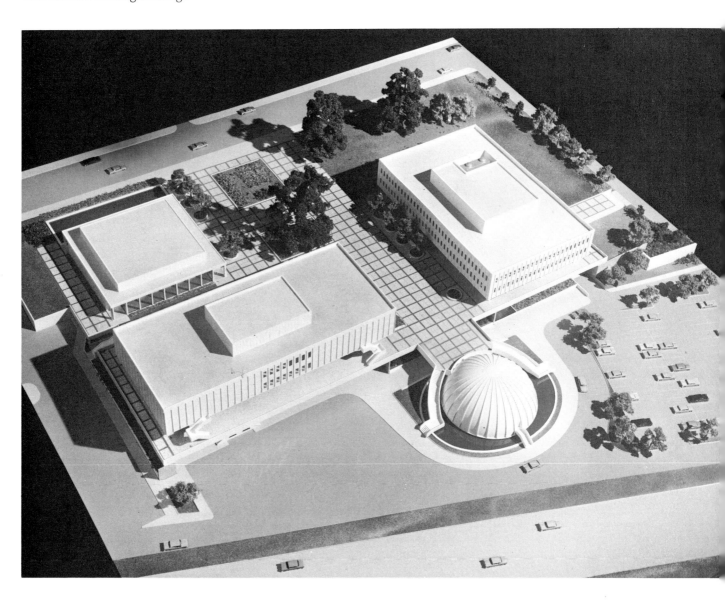

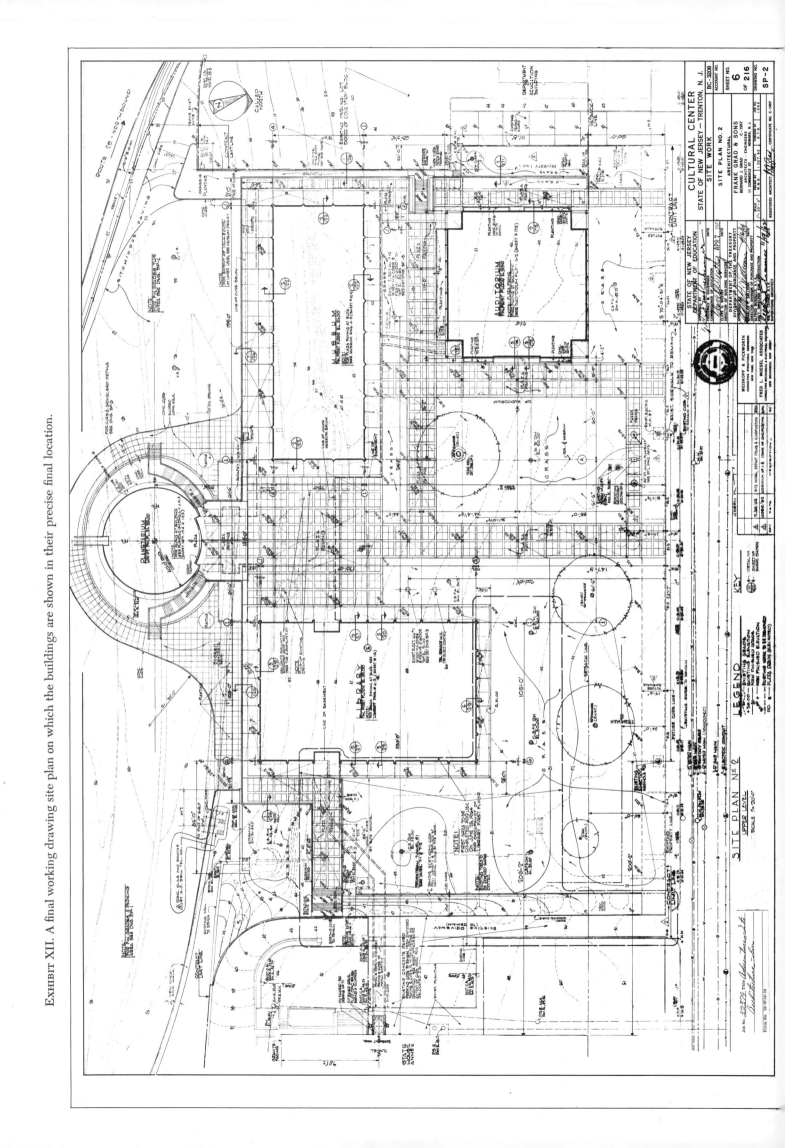

Exhibit XII. A final working drawing site plan on which the buildings are shown in their precise final location.

Exhibit XIII. A final working drawing of the first floor plan of the museum.

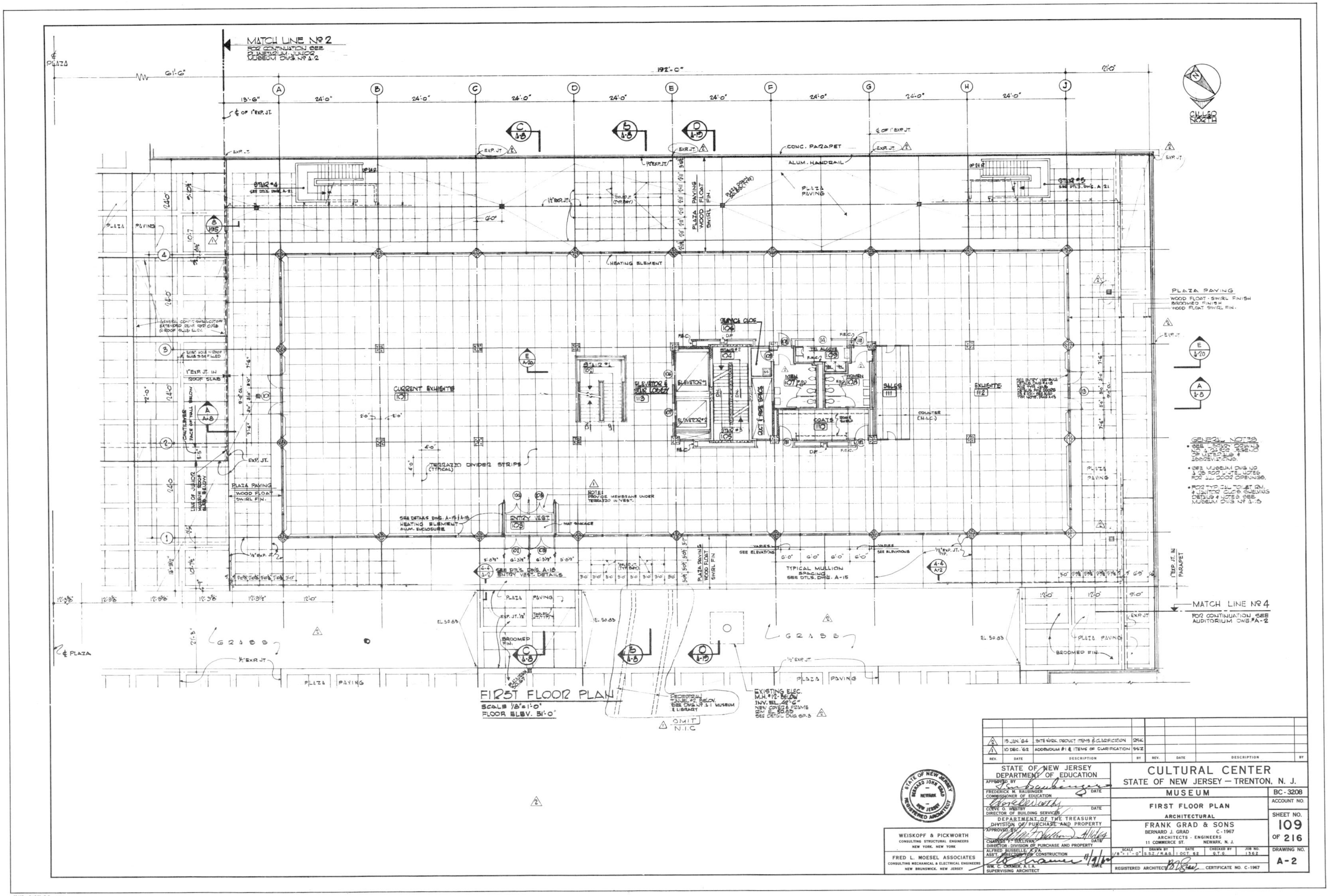

Exhibit XIV. A final working drawing of the first floor plan of the library.

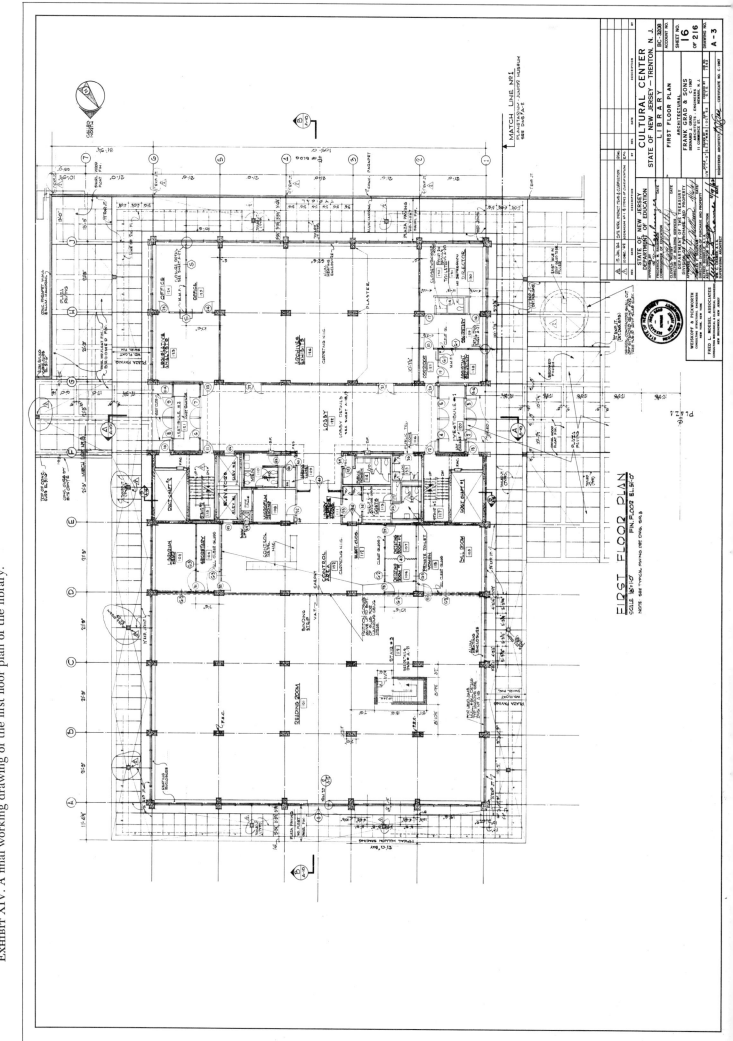

EXHIBIT XV. Building cross-sections of the museum.

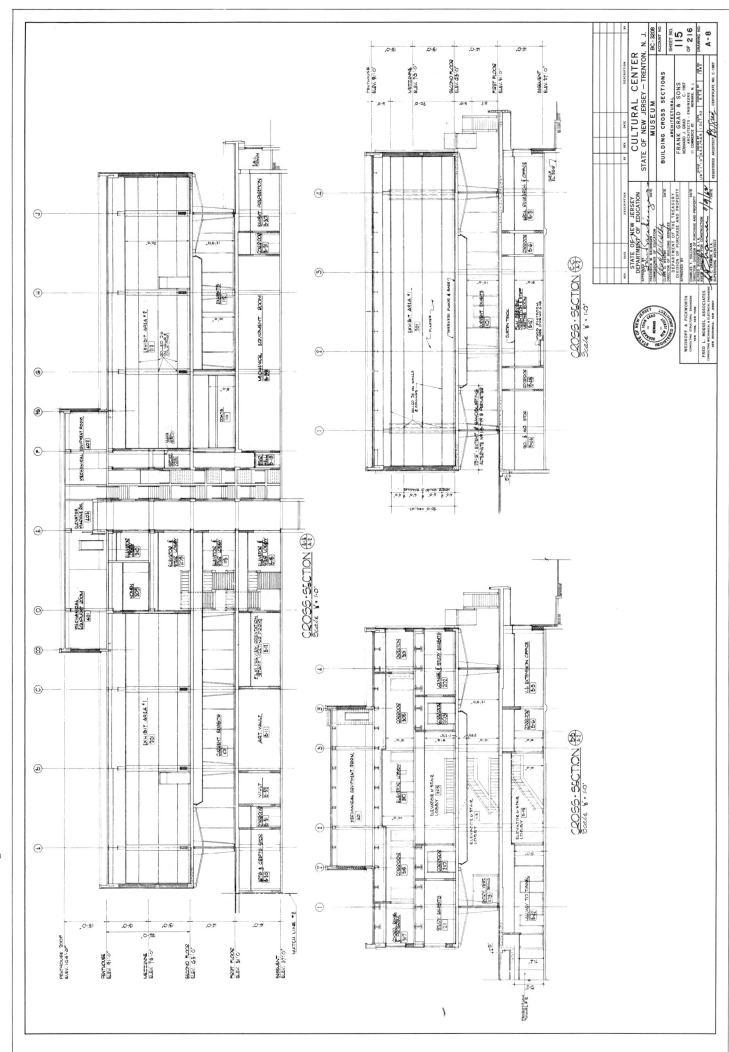

Exhibit XVI. A structural steel final working drawing of the second floor plan of the museum.

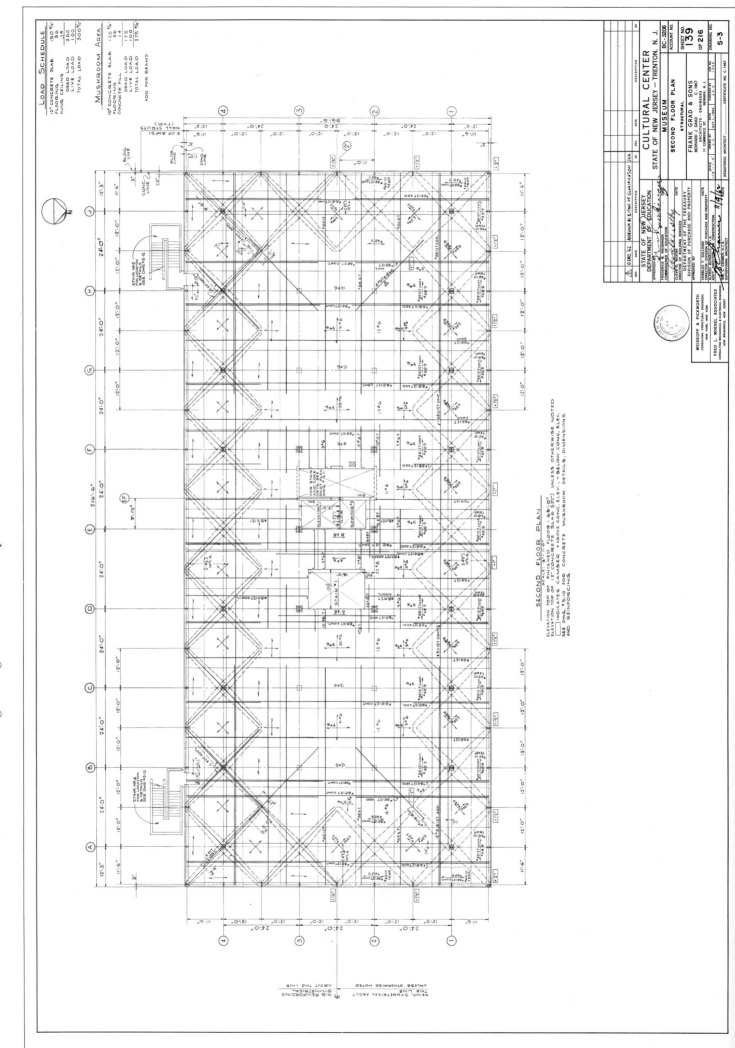

Exhibit XVII. A final working drawing of the museum and mezzanine floor plan, showing the HVAC systems.

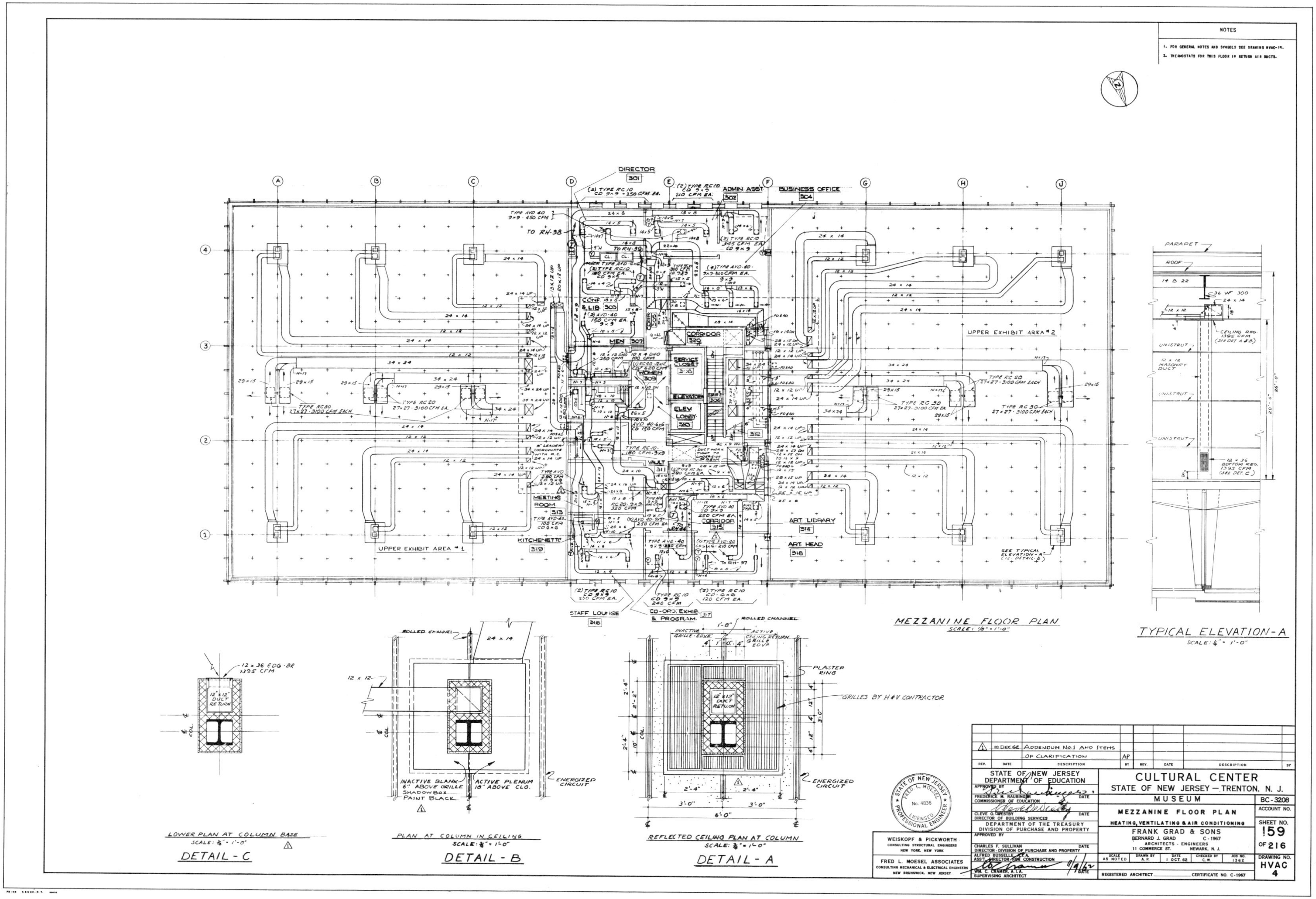

Exhibit XVIII. A first-floor plan of the museum showing the final electrical layout.

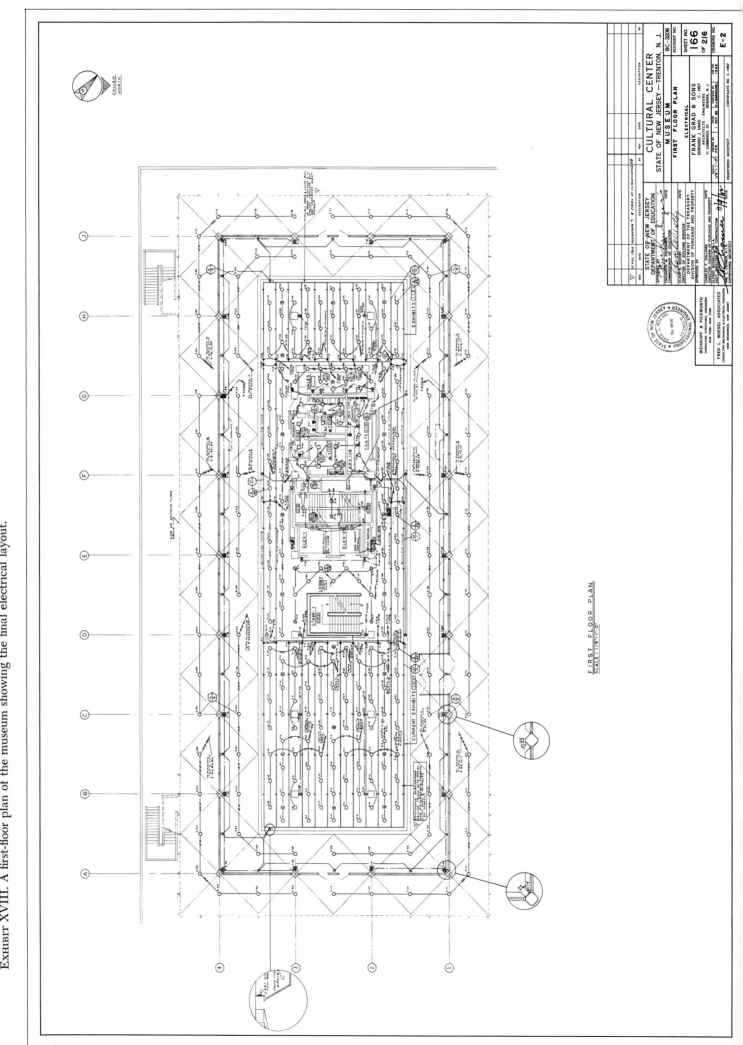

FIRST FLOOR PLAN
SCALE: 1/8"=1'-0"

EXHIBIT XIX. A cross-section and detail drawing of the planetarium.

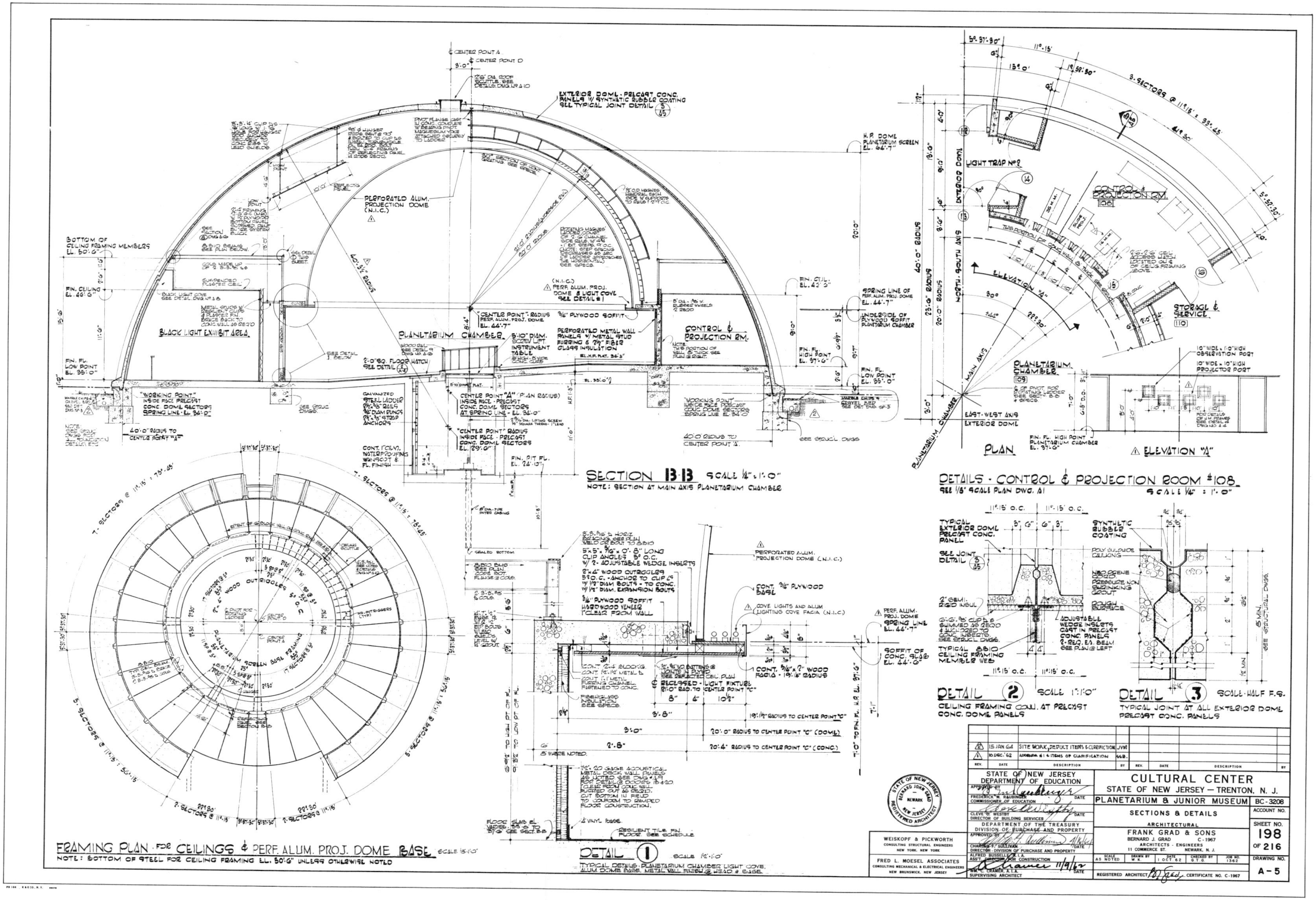

EXHIBIT XX. The south and west elevations of the museum in final working drawings.

Below

EXHIBIT XXI. A shop drawing showing marble details on the museum.

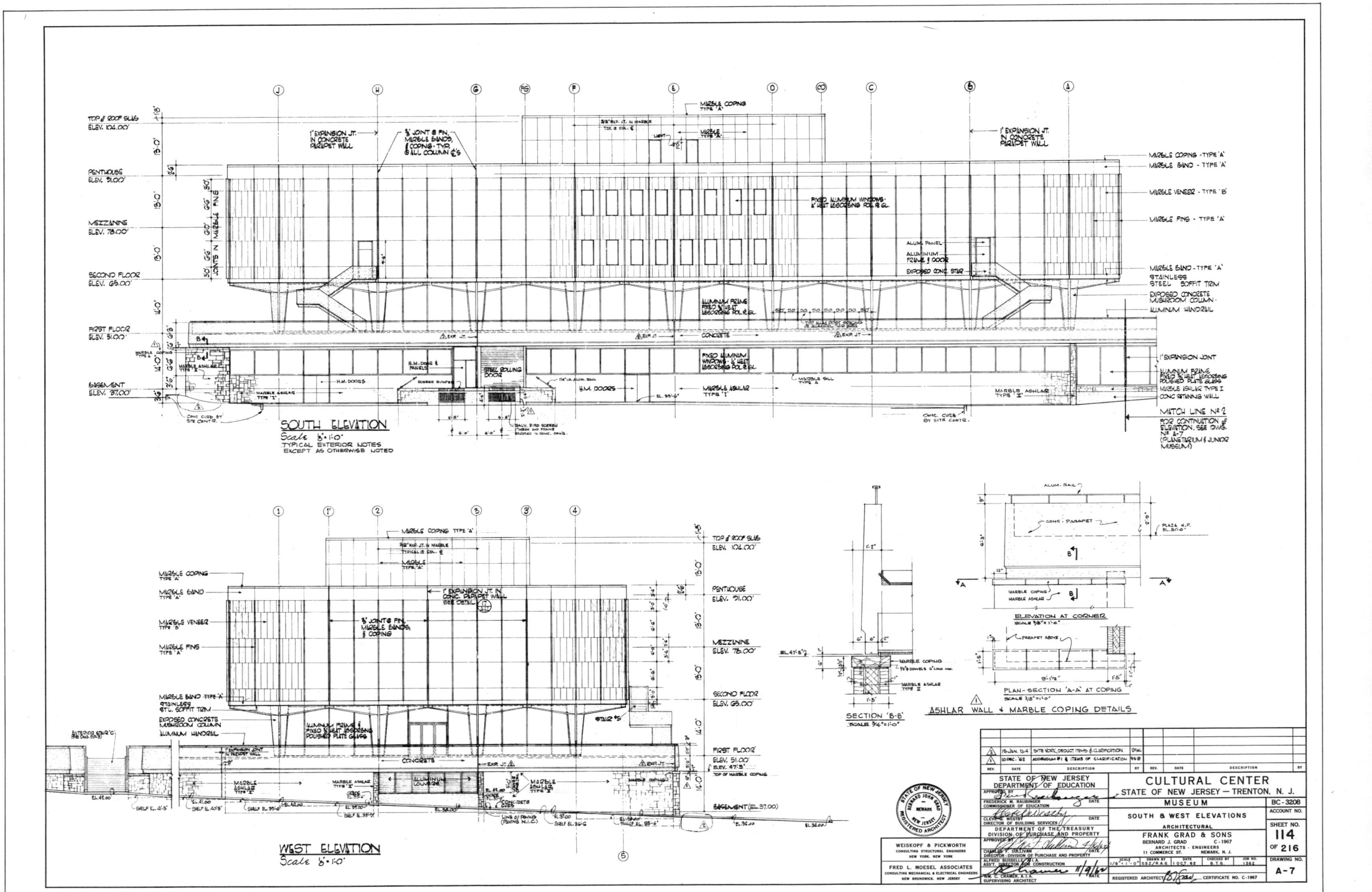

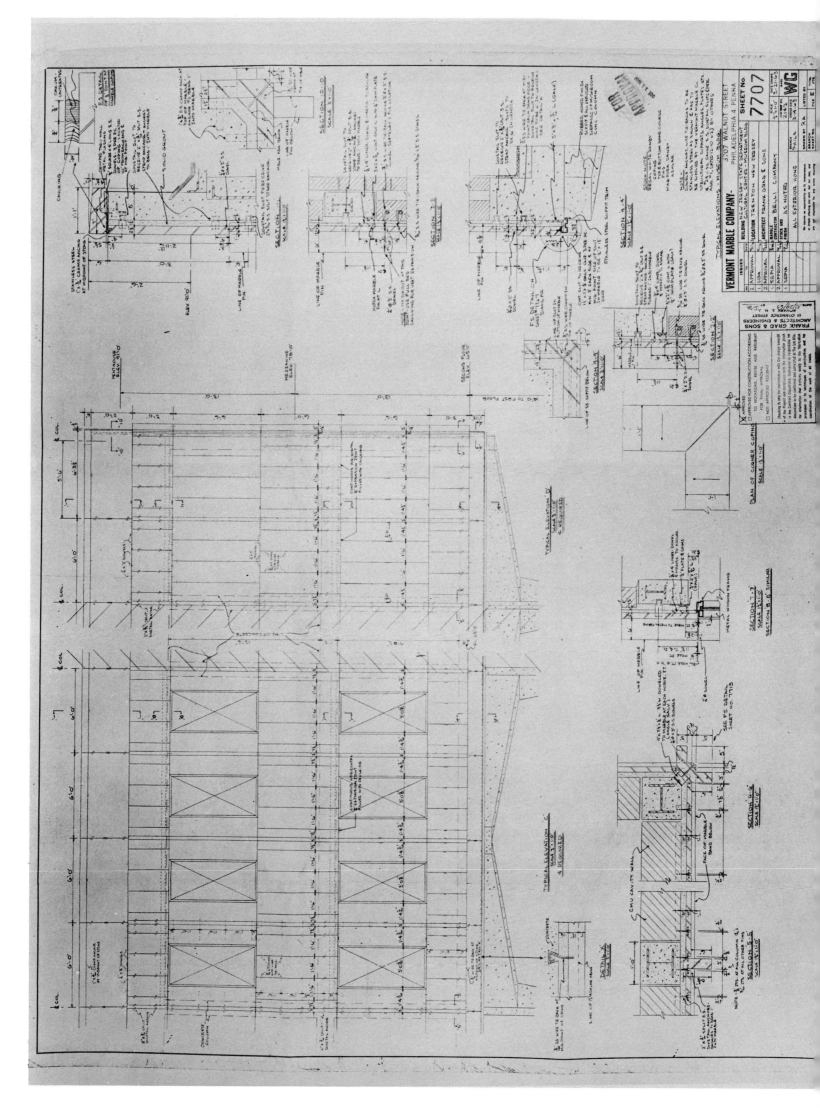

VERMONT MARBLE COMPANY

SHEET NO. 7707

-TYPICAL ELEVATIONS - MUSEUM BLDG.

Exhibit XXII. A photo of the model, looking at the project from John Fitch Way.

Exhibit XXIII. A photo of the model looking east.

Exhibit XXIV. An actual photo from the same point showing the finished building.

Exhibit XXV. An actual photo of the project looking east.

Exhibit XXVI. The interior of the planetarium.

Exhibit XXVII. A photo of the interior of the library showing a portion of the archives exhibit room.

Aerial view of the overall model, prepared for the State Capitol Development Commission, showing the disposition of existing and proposed State Buildings along the Delaware River.

drawings and contract specifications were completed and approved and the project sent out for bid. Three months later, bids were received, contracts evaluated and let; and construction was begun early in 1963. The summer of 1965 saw completion and acceptance of the project.

Exhibits XXII, XXIII, XXIV and XXV are examples of the happy ending to every architect's dream—it does not always come true. It is extremely difficult in this case to determine which is the model and which is the photograph. When brick and mortar in reality match the substance of his concept, the architect feels that he has really succeeded.

For those who enjoy statistics, the final working drawings consisted of 216 drawings and were made up of 81 architectural drawings, 42 structural drawings, 25 plumbing drawings, 32 HVAC drawings, 22 electrical drawings, 14 miscellaneous drawings. The contract specifications were contained in a book consisting of 624 pages.

9. The Challenge of Change

During my third year at the University of Pennsylvania, I took a course in watercolor painting. One afternoon I was alone in an alcove of the university museum, working on a watercolor of a marble Greek head. I had already spent more than twelve hours on the painting, but still I felt discontented with it. A tap on my shoulder startled me, and I turned to see Dr. George Walter Dawson, who headed the department of painting. He asked me whether I had ever known that it took two men to paint a picture. I did not know what he meant.

"Grad," he explained, "it takes one man to paint a picture and another to hit him on the head when he's finished. You finished that watercolor a long time ago. Go on to the next."

In more than three decades as an architect, I have had innumerable corroborations of Dr. Dawson's advice. I have learned to become both men required for any creative work—the man who undertakes it and the man who tells him when he has finished.

Just as it takes two men to paint a picture, it requires two parties to create a fine building, the right kind of architect and the right kind of client. Both are in short supply and, for the sake of our future environments, it is essential that both become more numerous. Our universities are turning out approximately 2,500 architects a year—a pitifully inadequate number. The dearth cannot be remedied immediately. Schools lack the funds for faculty and physical plant, and many promising students haven't the money for six or seven years of full-time study; for architecture is a discipline that does not lend itself to part-time schooling. Although many more schools are offering architectural curricula, the growth of architectural training and the establishment of architectural scholarships are two areas to which both the profession and the government should afford material assistance.

The role of government is especially important as society grows more complex. Many leaders in government are increasingly aware of the importance of architecture in the life of the nation. For too long, as August Heckscher pointed out in a recent speech, Americans tended to think that "art resided only in forms recognized by tradition and patronized by an elite." Government, he emphasized, has a responsibility that goes beyond efficiency and integrity. "It fulfills its true functions only when it acts with a sense of excellence and a concern for esthetic values. Concern with the arts should be taken as a natural and continuing interest of government." *

This philosophy, to which the late President Kennedy gave full support, repudiates the puritanical heritage that all but banished esthetics from public works and exalted the practical. If the federal government continues to foster good architecture, state and municipal governments will follow its pattern, and eventually these examples will persuade even the most recalcitrant and indifferent in the nation. It is not merely to undo the ugliness of our cities that architects and laymen are embracing this philosophy. It is, above all, because good planning and sensible investment in good design mean a more workable and satisfactory environment for all of us. To attain this goal, however, it is essential to establish better communications between architects, planners, and clients. If the good architect is to utilize his skills and talents, the client must have the incentive and discernment to commission distinguished work. Fine buildings, like fine paintings and fine sculpture, have always resulted from close collaboration between clients and architects.

The genius of America is manifested in our ability to invent and improvise. We have reshaped our governmental structure to lead us out of a catastrophic depression. When world democracy was challenged, almost overnight we retooled our economy to change from a peacetime machine to the world's greatest arsenal. We enjoy the most sophisticated technology that civilization has ever developed. In short, America has a talent for responding to dramatic and drastic changes.

At the same time we continue to countenance unbelievable

* *Design in the Federal Government*, 1965.

PENNSYLVANIA AVENUE PLAN, WASHINGTON, D.C. Aerial photo of
model looking northwest shows the proposed development along
Pennsylvania Avenue.
Photo by Dwain Faubion

NATIONAL AIR AND SPACE MUSEUM, WASHINGTON, D.C. Departure from the traditional type of government architecture and from the classic approach to museum design. Architect: Hellmuth, Obata & Kassabaum; Mills, Petticord & Mills.

poverty in all of our metropolitan communities. Every American city contains glaring reminders of our former unwillingness to meet the challenge of social responsibility. Our failures have been caused by our lack of planning. The state of crisis and decay evident in our cities are prime examples of where we have not used our talents in developing long-range planning concepts.

Most of our cities were not planned. They grew through the demands of a transient population. Each sector of a city's economy moved in its own direction, focusing on its own goal for its own self-interest, rather than for the common good.

For the first time in the history of mankind, people are fleeing from the cities in search of safety. Until recently, man has migrated to urban centers where he might find a haven of safety. Now the process has been reversed. Our decayed cities have lost their attraction, and what was once excitement is now peril.

What is needed now is a regeneration and planning on a huge scale to restore grace and delight to our cities. Only then will they attract business, commerce, professionals, the arts, and people of all walks of life to environments that are planned for safety, beauty and in consonance with human scale.

To this end, government and business must join forces with architects, engineers, planners, tax experts, and sociologists in a massive venture to replace dead and decaying slums with new physical facilities.

An outstanding example of such unity of purpose is the urban renewal project in Hartford, Connecticut, known as Constitution Plaza. This project, sponsored by the Travelers Insurance Company, produced a financially and esthetically satisfying example of architectural planning. However, such results are not likely to arise out of

situations in which clients' representatives refuse to approve architects' plans. Our cities suffer in too many instances from faceless architecture, which is the result of the dilution of ideas and the weakening of concepts. Decisions must be made by men of courage and not left to the anonymous "they" upon whom the blame is placed for rejection and inaction.

The Hartford experience had the distinguished precedent set by New York's Rockefeller Center, which is recognized throughout the world as a monument in the business-building concept, and it is being repeated in many cities. Far-sighted clients and capable architects have produced such projects as Pittsburgh's Golden Triangle, Philadelphia's Penn Center, Detroit's Gratiot Project, Chicago's urban revitalization, and the rebirth of Boston's central business district.

CONSTITUTION PLAZA, HARTFORD, CONNECTICUT. Architect: Charles DuBose.

Photo by Joseph W. Molitor

Views of an extremely well-planned and coordinated commercial urban renewal project. Constructed on what was once the site of a warehouse and second-rate industrial facilities, it provides Hartford with a commercial and architectural success story.

MIDTOWN AREA, NEW YORK CITY. The metropolis that
grew, and grew, and grows . . .
Photo by Gil Amiaga

GOVERNMENT CENTER, BOSTON, MASSACHUSETTS. Urban renewal complex now rising in downtown Boston to replace a once blighted area.
Photo by Aerial Photos of New England

On opposite page

ROCKEFELLER CENTER, NEW YORK CITY. The grandfather of all urban renewal projects. Begun in the Depression early in the '30's, it set the pattern for successful advance planning, coordinated design, and financial return.
Photo by Thomas Airviews

Penn Center, Philadelphia (before). Aerial view looking west from City Hall to the 30th Street Station showing the "China Wall" formed by the Pennsylvania Railroad.
Courtesy of Philadelphia Planning Commission

Philadelphia is probably the most dramatic example of what can happen to a decayed inner city when a coalition of forces with a common goal plans properly. The "Philadelphia Story" tells a tale of a city which was once strangled by railroad lines running from West Philadelphia into the center of the city. For the past sixteen years,

PENN CENTER, PHILADELPHIA (AFTER). Recent photo showing the removal of
the "China Wall" which made possible this vital commercial development.
Photo by Aero Service

hundreds of millions of dollars have been invested in an area called
Penn Center, a newly created urban development made possible by
the removal of Philadelphia's old "Chinese Wall." The result is a
new central city, successful and vital.

Two other projects worthy of note which fall into the category

THE CHALLENGE OF CHANGE   *173* of "new cities" in our country are Columbia City, which lies between Baltimore and Washington, and Irvine, which is in the San Diego, California area. Both are outstanding examples of the creative vision so necessary to the revitalization of our country.

Those renewal projects, which have already been completed, prove that this effort can be accomplished at a profit—rather than as

INDEPENDENCE HALL, PHILADELPHIA. One of America's historic buildings completely swallowed up by the surrounding commercial development.

an act of corporate charity; because there is a market for this concept.

In September, 1965, *Scientific American* devoted a whole issue to the problems of the world's cities. It would be futile to attempt a brief synopsis of this broad and penetrating discussion; however, I will touch on some of the most salient facts which are brought out in

INDEPENDENCE HALL, PHILADELPHIA. Facing on the new Mall, opening up the vista from all sides. Architect: Harbeson, Hough, Livingston & Larson.
Photo by Lawrence S. Williams, Inc.

HABITAT '67, MONTREAL. Innovative concept for prefabricated multi-family living quarters exhibited at Canada's World's Fair, EXPO '67. Architect: Moshe Safdie.
Photo by Gil Amiaga

On opposite page

PLACE VILLE MARIE, MONTREAL, CANADA. Skillful use of the articulated window-wall pattern in a large office building project. Architect: I. M. Pei & Partners.
Photo by Joseph W. Molitor

Right

PITTSBURGH'S GOLDEN TRIANGLE. Lying at the confluence of the Monongahela and Allegheny rivers, this complex shows the results of sound investment and professional planning.
Photo by Aerial Map Service Company

FARSTA CENTRUM, STOCKHOLM. Mid-city shopping center in Stockholm, well designed for the convenience of the pedestrian shopper.
Courtesy of Swedish Information Service

On opposite page

CHICAGO'S NORTH SIDE. View of the many projects which have been constructed in Chicago's renewal area.
Photo by Airpix

the seminar—points which are of prime importance especially to young people contemplating the study of architecture.

The world's population has doubled since 1940; the highest rate of increase has been in the underdeveloped countries where city services cannot be created fast enough to meet the needs of the swelling masses. According to the projections of the Bureau of the Census, the population of the New York Metropolitan area will reach twenty-one million by 1985, and thirty million by 2010. Projections by the United Nations indicate that by the year 2000, Calcutta, India, will have sixty-six million inhabitants.

The probable growth of the population in the United States will require the duplication of every building now in existence; but this enormous building program must begin now. Without proper planning, and co-ordination among all the parties in this awesome venture, all of our past mistakes will be duplicated as well, and we shall destroy ourselves materially and esthetically.

An editorial in *The New York Times*,* entitled "Man vs. Nature," discussed still another aspect of our contemporary crisis:

Earth's capacity to support human life is finite. If that limit is exceeded, vast disasters could result—and some of these disasters are not far off. . . . *Sports Illustrated* devoted much of a recent issue to an in-

* *The New York Times,* January 1, 1968.

WORLD TRADE CENTER. Two 110-story towers dominate the main entrance plaza surrounded by four separate low-lying buildings: United States Customs (right rear), World Trade Information Center and Hotel (left rear), Southeast Plaza (left foreground), and Northeast Plaza (right foreground). Architect: Minoru Yamasaki & Associates; Emery Roth & Sons.
Courtesy of Port of New York Authority

On opposite page, top

SYDNEY OPERA HOUSE, AUSTRALIA. This exciting concept has stirred much controversy with its spectacular roof of light and suspended concrete shells, above a massive but simple three-story building. Architect: Joern Utzon.
Courtesy of "Master Builders Magazine"

On opposite page, bottom

TECHCRETE, LEWIS WHARL PROJECT, BOSTON. Proposed project will utilize a new systems approach for multifamily housing. Architect: Carl Koch & Associates, Inc.
Photo by George Zimberg

SAN FRANCISCO, CALIFORNIA. Vast, dynamic urban renewal program.
Photo by Clyde Sunderland. Courtesy of "Architectural Forum"

NEW CITY CORE, FORT WORTH. Gruen plan for the redevelopment and transformation of the downtown area into a pedestrian island, ringed by expressways and six huge garages.
Photo by Gordon Sommers

cisive examination of the pillaging of the environment and its consequences. The magazine concluded that the engineers' tyranny over the environment must be ended. "Putting an engineer in charge of a resource such as a river basin is no smarter than hiring a plumber to design a fountain."

The challenges that are being created today will be met by teams of experts—planners, engineers, sociologists, economists, and anthropologists. Co-ordinating the efforts of these specialists should be the function of architects.

In contemplating the challenges of tomorrow, we have only to review the fantastic advances which have been made in science and technology during the past forty years: the unleashing and harnessing of atomic energy; supersonic flight; and man's penetration of outer space.

Confronted by the gigantic problems of population explosion and the preservation of natural resources, will the architect continue in his present role in the future?

To cope with these challenges, corporations are pooling their resources and manpower. Similarly, several architectural firms have merged with large corporations in accordance with the total team concept needed to tackle these complex problems.

Although some architects will continue to design individual buildings, the day of their involvement solely with single structures is rapidly ending.

On opposite page

NEWARK AIRPORT REDEVELOPMENT PROGRAM
Courtesy of Port of New York Authority
Overall site rendering and a detail of model for the proposed Newark Airport Redevelopment Program, sponsored by the Port of New York Authority and designed to incorporate the latest advances in air travel facilities.

The leaders of the architectural profession will adopt the total team concept in coping with the problems of rebuilding entire business districts and creating new cities and towns. Architecture of tomorrow will embrace the solution of sociological and behavioral patterns as well as the traditional aspects of structural, transportational, and personal design concepts.

Throughout the country, young men are advancing bold new concepts. Even their elders are shedding the petty jealousies of an earlier era in the profession when the exchange of ideas and design

MODERN RESIDENTIAL AREA, GOTHENBURG.
Photo by Stig Sjöstedt Reklamfoto.
Courtesy of Swedish Information Service

A comparison in the contemporary idiom of multi-family housing; one
in Massachusetts for Harvard's married students and the other in
Gothenburg, Sweden, for general residential facilities.

concepts with colleagues—and competitors—was rare indeed.

Today, because of their nationwide association in the AIA, with
its various commissions and committees, and with the growth of
joint ventures, architects are being brought much closer together.
They exchange ideas freely, even on internal operations; a generation ago this would have been unthinkable.

The young person who elects to enter this profession has the
assurance that the experience and knowledge of every colleague is
available to assist him.

THE CHALLENGE OF CHANGE   *189*

A panoramic view of the proposal for lower Manhattan prepared by senior students of Pratt Institute. This provocative study of lower Manhattan is indicative of the thinking of the new generation of young architects. The students were assisted by members of the faculty under the direction of Dean Olindo Grossi.

Photo courtesy of Pratt Institute

In conclusion, the graduates of the late 1960's have a certainty of taking their places in a world far different from the one I entered in the Depression era of the early 1930's. I had the inestimable good luck to be the son of a practicing architect who could afford to hire me at $35 a week. A few months later, I had the stunning experience of walking into a Schrafft's restaurant for a soda and being served by a fellow graduate in architecture. America at that time had little use and less money for architects. Today's affluent American society needs good architects and is ready to reward their talents and skills.

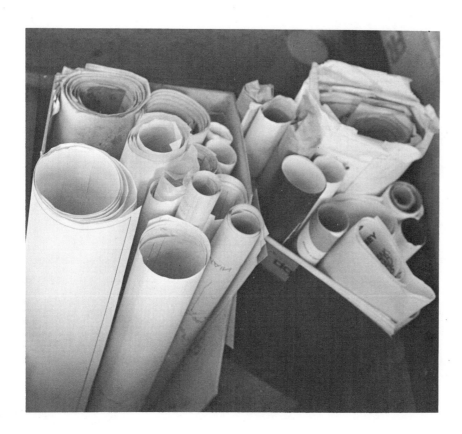